THE
VIRGIN
MARKETER

Noel Capon

Graduate School of Business
Columbia University
New York, NY

www.axcesscapon.com

Library of Congress Cataloging-in-Publication Data

Capon, Noel
  The Virgin Marketer / Noel Capon
    p. cm.
  ISBN: 978-0-9833300-7-3
    1. Virgin Marketer, The.   I. Title: The Virgin Marketer.   II. Noel Capon

Editor: Lyn Maize
Copy Editor: Christy Goldfinch
Book / Cover Design: Anna Botelho

DEDICATION

To the countless executives around
the world who have developed
successful marketing plans for
their companies using *The Virgin
Marketer* or similar approaches.

ABOUT THE AUTHOR

NOEL CAPON is the R. C. Kopf Professor of International Marketing and past Chair of the Marketing Division at the Graduate School of Business, Columbia University. Educated primarily in Great Britain, Professor Capon earned B.Sc. and Ph.D. degrees in Chemistry from University College, London University. He also received degrees in Business Administration from Manchester (Dip. BA), Harvard (MBA), and Columbia Business School (Ph.D.).

Professor Capon joined the Columbia Business School faculty in 1979. Previously he served on the faculty of, and received tenure from, the University of California – Graduate School of Management, UCLA. He has taught and held faculty positions at Harvard Business School; Australia — Monash University; England — Bradford Management Centre and Manchester Business School; France — INSEAD; Hong Kong — The Hong Kong University of Science and Technology (HKUST); China — China European International Business School (CEIBS — Shanghai); and India — Indian School of Business (ISB — Hyderabad). Professor Capon currently holds the position of Distinguished Visiting Professor at Manchester Business School.

Professor Capon has published more than 60 refereed articles and book chapters, and is editor for sections on Marketing, and Sales Management and Distribution, in the *AMA Management Handbook* (1994). He has published more than 20 books, including *Corporate Strategic Planning*, a major study of the planning practices of major U.S. manufacturing corporations (Columbia University Press 1988); *The Marketing of Financial Services: A Book of Cases* (Prentice-Hall 1992); *Planning the Development of Builders, Leaders, and Managers of Twenty First Century Business* (Kluwer Academic Publishers 1996) on the curriculum review process at Columbia Business School; *Why Some Firms Perform Better than Others: Towards a More Integrative Explanation* (Kluwer Academic Publishers 1996) on the underpinnings of superior corporate financial performance; *The Asian Marketing Case Book* (Prentice Hall 1999); *Marketing Management in the 21st Century* (Prentice Hall 2001); *Key Account Management and Planning* (Free Press 2001); *Total Integrated Marketing* (Free Press 2003); *The Marketing Mavens* (Crown Business 2007); *Managing Global Accounts* (Wessex 2008); *Strategic Account Strategy* (Wessex 2011); and *Sales Eats First* (Wessex 2011).

In addition to *Managing Marketing in the 21st Century* (U.S. and European editions), Professor Capon's textbook publications include *Capon's Marketing Framework* (Wessex 2009); a companion marketing planning workbook, *The Virgin Marketer* (Wessex 2007); and several Student Study Guides. Professor Capon's textbooks are also published in Chinese, Russian, and Spanish.

Professor Capon contributes extensively to Columbia Business School's Executive Education. He is the Founding Director of *Managing Strategic Accounts* and the *Global Account Manager Certification* program in conjunction with St. Gallen University (Switzerland). He teaches on Columbia's *Full-time MBA and Executive MBA* (EMBA) programs and its partner program with London Business School. He founded and directs the Advanced Marketing Management Program in conjunction with the Chinese European International Business School (CEIBS — Shanghai). He also designs, directs, and teaches in numerous custom programs for major corporations globally. In 2001, Professor Capon co-founded *The Chief Sales Executive Forum*, offering multiple educational opportunities for sales leaders.

PREFACE

The Virgin Marketer is a companion volume to two textbooks: *Managing Marketing in the 21st Century (MM21C)* and *Capon's Marketing Framework (CMF)*. As you read and study the material in your textbook, we hope that you will learn a lot about marketing. But no matter how much effort you put into your text, and how good a job we have done with *MM21C* and *CMF*, that is really only a start. You will only begin to live and breathe the marketing philosophy by getting your hands dirty and actually *doing* marketing. That is the purpose of *The Virgin Marketer (TVM)*.

The material in *TVM* has a very long pedigree, with many well-known domestic and multi-national firms having used selections and/or variations of the frameworks to develop actionable marketing plans. In its current version, *TVM* has guided the development of marketing plans for well over 30 organizations, large and small. These organizations are listed in Appendix 1.

In the chapters that follow, we guide you though the marketing process, from insight to action. For each chapter in your textbook, there is a parallel chapter in *TVM*. In *MM21C* and *CMF*, we describe marketing in terms of marketing as a philosophy, six marketing imperatives that encompass the job of strategic marketing, four marketing principles, and the insights each marketer must secure to be successful. We use many examples that best describe each of the important ideas. In *TVM*, you, the reader, choose the firm, business unit, or other organization that is most interesting or meaningful to you. We want you to select a marketing case to try out your new knowledge, so that you can develop and hone your marketing skills. We designed the material in Appendix 2 to also help you enhance your own intellectual capital.

CHOOSING A MARKETING CASE

In choosing your marketing case, you have a broad set of possibilities. For a start, you may consider any number of corporations we discuss in your textbook, like Virgin. Under Sir Richard Branson's leadership, Virgin has become one of the world's most well-known and respected brands for business and philanthropy and has plans for space travel and global warming research. But beneath the corporate brand are a host of diverse businesses in many different industries, from Virgin Atlantic Airways to Virgin Mobile. We suggest you consider choosing a Virgin business for your marketing case.

Another approach is to identify a firm/business unit you are familiar with. Maybe you can choose one where you work, or would like to work. As you complete the various exercises in *TVM*, you will learn a tremendous amount about the strategies of your chosen firm/business unit, its markets, and the industries where it competes. If you already have a marketing position, then completing the marketing case will actually be doing your job! If you are going to enter the job market, then working through *TVM* will provide you an advantage. By completing the marketing case, you will be able to demonstrate your knowledge and expertise to executives seeking high-caliber human resources for their firm and/or business unit.

Your professor may have suggestions for a firm/business unit to use as a marketing case. The professor may have company contacts who can provide you good access to data/information and/or executives to help you. We believe the learning you gain from completing your marketing case will be highly valuable for the firm/business unit you study.

Finally, you can simply select a product/service of interest to you that is already on the market, or even a product/service yet to reach market. In either case, the data difficulties will be greater, but that is no reason not to take this route. You may even use the marketing case to investigate your own ideas for an entrepreneurial startup

WORKING THROUGH THE CHAPTERS

We suggest that you work through each chapter in *TVM* as you complete each chapter in *MM21C/CMF*. Not only will this make each activity more fresh and relevant, but it will avoid pushing off data gathering and analysis to the end of the semester. Your professor will be your guide, but here are a few tips for getting the most out of your *Virgin Marketer* project.

The best data are often obtained directly from your chosen firm/business unit. If you do not have direct access to company executives, then you will have to use external sources. The Internet in general, and Google or other search engines in particular, can take you a long way in collecting basic data. After all, you are certainly in far better shape than your peers of just a decade ago! Another online source is the digital library at your school or company. Libraries often have access to subscription-based business databases like Factiva, LexisNexis, and Dun & Bradstreet. Sometimes, if you want data on firm/business unit customers and competitors, you may approach this challenge the old-fashioned way — talk directly to a few customers, conduct a customer DILO (day in the life of) or focus group, or administer a small survey.

Regardless, you will never have all the data you need to complete your marketing case. But don't let that stop you. Sometimes you will just have to make an assumption and move forward. Just focus on your marketing case, and *TVM* will help you learn a systematic process for the art and science of marketing. Here are a few tips for working through *TVM*:

- In each chapter there are frameworks. We often present these frameworks in the form of templates to fill out. But you must remember that the purpose of including a particular framework is *not just* to fill out the template. The template is a way to help you formulate good questions and to organize your ideas. The real value is the thought you put into the topic. If you are working in a small group, the conversation among group members will be especially valuable.

- In many cases, the frameworks we ask you to work with in later chapters rely on completed work from earlier chapters. For example, you cannot do a decent job of marketing implementation unless you have formulated a market strategy.

- Some of the frameworks may not apply to your marketing case. For example, if you use a sales force for your entire promotional effort, questions about the advertising budget would not be relevant.

We designed *TVM* for use in profit-seeking firms. Some of you will be interested in public or not-for-profit organizations. The frameworks are very useful for these situations, but you may need to do a little reframing to fit the particular circumstances of the organization you choose.

STRUCTURING THE FINAL REPORT

For the final report, you gather together all the learning you gained while working through the *The Virgin Marketer* chapters. *TVM* provides the structure for writing a clear, concise, and professional business report where you present your analysis and recommendations. As you prepare the report, you should put yourself in the reader's shoes. Present your work clearly and logically, so that the reader can easily understand what is going on. Here are a few tips:

- Take the time to interpret for the reader the results within the various templates. A filled-out template, with little or no explanation of what the data actually means, is useless.

- Include your analyses within the body of the report, rather than putting them at the back in an appendix. As always, we defer to your professor for his/her preferred format.

- A report should always have an executive summary. This gives the reader (often an executive) a one- or two-page overview of what to expect, a project summary, and your key recommendations. We present some ideas for structuring the executive summary right before the appendices.

- Following the executive summary, provide the reader with background in the form of a preamble. A preamble is a type of introduction that frames your entire report by introducing the firm/business unit and broadly identifying the product/market arena under consideration. If the technology is novel, give the reader a short primer on how the product/service works. Use the preamble to provide background information so the reader can understand how the product/market arena relates to other firm products/markets. We walk through ideas for structuring the preamble.

- If the professor assigns the marketing case as a group effort, and one member has specific information about the firm/business unit or topic, say so in the preamble. If you are working as a group, the preamble can double as a briefing document for other team members.

- Don't forget to acknowledge those who helped you with your marketing case.

Now you are ready to get started on your marketing case. Good luck as *The Virgin Marketer* guides you through your project!

In preparing for battle, I have always found that plans are useless, but planning is indispensable.

— General Dwight D. Eisenhower

TABLE OF CONTENTS

PREAMBLE

The main purpose of the preamble is to state the topic of your marketing case in a way that frames your analysis and recommendations. You should state very broadly the product/market arena you are addressing.

Here is where you provide background on your chosen firm/business unit. Depending on the focus, you may provide corporate level and/or business unit information. If your marketing case is a startup, some of the following items do not apply. You must make your own decisions.

Information that you should provide in the preamble includes:

- **Product/market arena**
  - The product/product line you are considering: how it works, how customers use it
  - Broadly defined, the market for the product/product line
- **Background to the firm/business unit**
  - Size information: for example, revenues, assets, employees, budgets
  - Organizational outputs: products/services
  - Organizational inputs: capital equipment, raw materials, human resources
  - Technologies employed
  - Employee skill levels
  - Organizational design: how various departments are related; who reports to whom. If possible, include an organization chart.
  - Recent significant corporate events: for example, acquisitions, divestitures, strategic alliances, lawsuits, leadership changes
  - Any other information you believe is pertinent to your marketing case
- Performance data for the previous few years — revenues, profits, stock price — Figure PA.1

The purpose of the preamble is not to disclose confidential information. Rather, it sets the stage for your analyses in the chapters that follow. The preamble provides the reader with a framework within which to evaluate those analyses.

FIGURE PA.1

HISTORICAL FINANCIAL RESULTS

	Year − 5	Year − 4	Year − 3	Year − 2	Year − 1
Sales Revenues					
Cost of Goods Sold					
Gross Profits					
Expenses					
Net Profits					
Assets					
Stock Price Range					
Number of Employees					

Managing Marketing in the 21ˢᵗ Century

SECTION I: MARKETING AND THE FIRM

CHAPTER 1
Introduction to Managing Marketing

CHAPTER 2
The Value of Customers

SECTION II: FUNDAMENTAL INSIGHTS FOR STRATEGIC MARKETING

CHAPTER 3
Market Insight

CHAPTER 4
Customer Insight

CHAPTER 5
Insight about Competitors, Company, and Complementers

CHAPTER 6
Marketing Research

TRANSITION TO STRATEGIC MARKETING

SECTION III: STRATEGIC MARKETING

IMPERATIVE 1
Determine and Recommend Which Markets to Address

CHAPTER 7
Identifying and Choosing Opportunities

IMPERATIVE 2
Identify and Target Market Segments

CHAPTER 8
Market Segmentation and Targeting

IMPERATIVE 3
Set Strategic Direction and Positioning

CHAPTER 9
Market Strategy: Integrating Firm Efforts for Marketing Success

CHAPTER 10
Managing through the Life Cycle

CHAPTER 11
Managing Brands

SECTION IV: IMPLEMENTING THE MARKET STRATEGY

IMPERATIVE 4
Design the Market Offer

PART A: PROVIDING CUSTOMER VALUE

PART B: COMMUNICATING CUSTOMER VALUE

PART C: DELIVERING CUSTOMER VALUE

PART D: GETTING PAID FOR CUSTOMER VALUE

CHAPTER 12
Managing the Product Line

CHAPTER 15
Integrated Marketing Communications

CHAPTER 18
Distribution Decisions

CHAPTER 19
Critical Underpinnings of Pricing Decisions

CHAPTER 13
Managing Services and Customer Service

CHAPTER 16
Mass and Digital Communication

CHAPTER 20
Setting Prices

CHAPTER 14
Developing New Products

CHAPTER 17
Directing and Managing the Field Sales Effort

IMPERATIVE 5
Secure Support from Other Functions

CHAPTER 21
Ensuring the Firm Implements the Market Offer as Planned

IMPERATIVE 6
Monitor and Control

CHAPTER 22
Monitoring and Controlling Firm Functioning and Performance

SECTION V: SPECIAL MARKETING TOPICS

CHAPTER 23
International, Regional, and Global Marketing

Section I: Marketing and the Firm

CHAPTER 1: INTRODUCTION TO MANAGING MARKETING

Now you have some ideas about marketing and understand the structure of your textbook, here are a few questions about Chapter 1 to get you started on your marketing case.

A. MARKETING AS A PHILOSOPHY: EXTERNAL AND INTERNAL ORIENTATIONS

If your product/service already exists, assess the responsible business unit rather than the entire firm. If you are planning a startup, think about your plans for the organization that will lead and manage the startup. Use one of the following instruments to assess the degree of internal/external orientation.

MARKOR METHOD FOR MEASURING INTERNAL/EXTERNAL ORIENTATION. The 20-item MARKOR scale — Figure 1A.1 — has three sections: *intelligence generation, intelligence dissemination,* and *responsiveness.*[1] Using a 1-to-7 scale, specify your level of agreement with the statements and examine the absolute and relative scores. Are you satisfied with the score for your firm/business unit? Are there major differences between the relative intelligence generation, intelligence dissemination, and responsiveness scores? How could your chosen organization unit improve on areas with low ratings? Where are the major leverage points to improve the degree of external orientation? What recommendations do you have for improving in areas with low ratings? If your marketing case is a startup, what steps should you take to build an external orientation from the very beginning?

COLOR: DIAGNOSTICS FOR MEASURING INTERNAL/EXTERNAL ORIENTATION. The COLOR approach to measuring the internal/external orientation balance examines the way your firm/business unit approaches key management issues. Nineteen issues are organized into seven categories:

- The planning system (5)
- Defining the market arena (3)
- Treatment of customers (3)
- Marketing spending (3)
- Product-line decisions (2)
- Cost to the customer (2)
- Business organization (1)

COLOR is based on these categories.[2] Apply COLOR — Figure 1A.2 — to your firm/business unit. For each pair of statements, rate your firm/business unit on a 1-to-7 scale.

What did you learn about your firm/business unit by completing COLOR? Where are the major leverage points to improve the degree of external orientation? What recommendations do you have for improving in areas with low ratings? If your marketing case is a start-up, what steps would you take to build an external orientation from the very beginning?

	I DO NOT AGREE AT ALL						I COMPLETELY AGREE
	1	2	3	4	5	6	7
1. In this business unit, we meet with customers at least once a year to find out what products or services they will need in the future.	❑	❑	❑	❑	❑	❑	❑
2. In this business unit we do a lot of in-house market research.	❑	❑	❑	❑	❑	❑	❑
3. We are slow to detect changes in our customers' product preferences.	❑	❑	❑	❑	❑	❑	❑
4. We poll end users at least once a year to assess the quality of our products and services.	❑	❑	❑	❑	❑	❑	❑
5. We are slow to detect fundamental shifts in our industry (for example, competition, technology, regulation).	❑	❑	❑	❑	❑	❑	❑
6. We periodically review the likely effects of changes in our business environment (for example, regulation) on customers.	❑	❑	❑	❑	❑	❑	❑
7. We have interdepartmental meetings at least once a quarter to discuss marketing trends and developments.	❑	❑	❑	❑	❑	❑	❑
8. Marketing personnel in our business unit spend time discussing customers' future needs with other functional departments.	❑	❑	❑	❑	❑	❑	❑
9. When something important happens to a major customer or market, the whole business unit knows about it within a short period.	❑	❑	❑	❑	❑	❑	❑
10. Data on customer satisfaction are disseminated at all levels in this business unit on a regular basis.	❑	❑	❑	❑	❑	❑	❑
11. When one department finds out something important about competitors, it is slow to alert other departments.	❑	❑	❑	❑	❑	❑	❑
12. It takes us forever to decide how to respond to our competitor's price changes.	❑	❑	❑	❑	❑	❑	❑
13. For one reason or another, we tend to ignore changes in our customers' product or service needs.	❑	❑	❑	❑	❑	❑	❑
14. We periodically review our product development efforts to ensure that they are in line with what customers want.	❑	❑	❑	❑	❑	❑	❑
15. Several departments get together periodically to plan a response to changes taking place in our business environment.	❑	❑	❑	❑	❑	❑	❑
16. If a major competitor were to launch an intensive campaign targeted at our customers, we would implement a response immediately.	❑	❑	❑	❑	❑	❑	❑
17. The activities of the different departments in this business unit are well coordinated.	❑	❑	❑	❑	❑	❑	❑
18. Customer complaints fall on deaf ears in this business unit.	❑	❑	❑	❑	❑	❑	❑
19. Even if we came up with a great marketing plan, we probably would not be able to implement it in a timely fashion.	❑	❑	❑	❑	❑	❑	❑
20. When we find that customers would like to modify a product or service, the departments involved make concerted efforts to do so.	❑	❑	❑	❑	❑	❑	❑

INSTRUCTIONS

1. Reverse code items 3, 5, 11, 12, 13, 18 and 19 by subtracting the figure you circled from 8: _____
   (Example: If you gave the item a rating of 2, the score should be 8–2 = 6.)
2. Add the scores of items 1 through 6. The total is your **intelligence generation** score: _____
3. Divide the score by 6 to get a relative score: _____
4. Add the scores of items 7 through 11. The total is your **intelligence dissemination** score: _____
5. Divide the score by 5 to get a relative score: _____
6. Add the scores of items 12 through 20. The total is your **responsiveness** score: _____
7. Divide the score by 9 to get a relative score: _____

FIGURE 1A.2

COLOR – A DIAGNOSTIC TOOL FOR MEASURING INTERNAL/EXTERNAL ORIENTATION

A. THE PLANNING SYSTEM

1. OBJECTIVE SETTING

	1	2	3	4	5	6	7	
Our objectives are set with a predominantly internal focus.	❏	❏	❏	❏	❏	❏	❏	We maintain a strong external focus in setting objectives.

2. PLANNING AND BUDGETING

	1	2	3	4	5	6	7	
Our plans comprise largely numerical budgets.	❏	❏	❏	❏	❏	❏	❏	Our plans are expressed largely in words.

3. GATHERING MARKET INFORMATION

	1	2	3	4	5	6	7	
We pay little attention to customer/competitor data gathering and analysis.	❏	❏	❏	❏	❏	❏	❏	We put major efforts into customer/competitor data gathering and analysis.

4. SALES FORECASTING

	1	2	3	4	5	6	7	
We do a terrible job of forecasting sales volume.	❏	❏	❏	❏	❏	❏	❏	We do a great job of forecasting sales volume.

5. INFORMATION SYSTEMS

	1	2	3	4	5	6	7	
We develop information systems to reduce costs and increase operating efficiency.	❏	❏	❏	❏	❏	❏	❏	We develop information systems so we can be more effective in the marketplace.

B. DEFINING THE MARKET ARENA

1. ATTITUDE TOWARD THE "RULES OF THE GAME"

	1	2	3	4	5	6	7	
We accept the rulings made by various legal and regulatory bodies.	❏	❏	❏	❏	❏	❏	❏	We actively work to make legal and regulatory rulings in our favor.

2. ATTITUDE TOWARD REGULATION

	1	2	3	4	5	6	7	
We actively dislike all forms of regulation.	❏	❏	❏	❏	❏	❏	❏	We have a fine-tuned sense of which regulations are good for the firm.

3. COMPETITIVE VIEW

	1	2	3	4	5	6	7	
We believe our competition comprises firms attempting to meet the same customer needs and wants as ourselves.	❏	❏	❏	❏	❏	❏	❏	We know our competition is other firms selling similar products and services.

C. TREATMENT OF CUSTOMERS

1. ATTITUDE TOWARD CUSTOMER SERVICE

	1	2	3	4	5	6	7	
Having to deliver customer service is a necessary evil.	❏	❏	❏	❏	❏	❏	❏	We believe that customer service is a crucial means of securing differential advantage.

2. ATTITUDE TOWARD PRODUCT/SERVICE DEFECTS

	1	2	3	4	5	6	7	
We believe in "buyer beware."	❏	❏	❏	❏	❏	❏	❏	We go out of our way to avoid any type of product defect.

3. ALLOCATION UNDER SCARCITY

	1	2	3	4	5	6	7	
When we have supply shortages, we use standard allocation formulae to allocate our capacity.	❏	❏	❏	❏	❏	❏	❏	When we have supply shortages, we make strategic allocation decisions.

CONTINUES ON NEXT PAGE

D. MARKETING SPENDING

	1	2	3	4	5	6	7	
1. ATTITUDE TOWARD MARKETING EXPENDITURES When prodits are under pressure, marketing budgets are the first to be cut.	❏	❏	❏	❏	❏	❏	❏	We regard our marketing budgets as investments in the business.
2. RESPONSE TO SHORTFALLS When we are under financial pressure, we cut budgets by the same percentage across the board.	❏	❏	❏	❏	❏	❏	❏	When we are under financial pressure, we make strategically focused budgeting decisions.
3. RESPONSE TO RECESSION In recessionary times, we cut our marketing budgets.	❏	❏	❏	❏	❏	❏	❏	In recessionary times, we tend to increase or hold firm our marketing budgets.

E. PRODUCT LINE DECISIONS

	1	2	3	4	5	6	7	
1. APPROACH TO PRODUCT DEVELOPMENT We have a haphazard approach to new product development.	❏	❏	❏	❏	❏	❏	❏	Our new product development procedures are clearly established and communicated.
2. PRODUCT LINE BREADTH Our product line is misbalanced (too narrow or too broad).	❏	❏	❏	❏	❏	❏	❏	We make careful product line choices to avoid too broad or too narrow a product line.

F. COST TO THE CUSTOMER

	1	2	3	4	5	6	7	
1. APPROACH TO SETTING PRICES We set prices on a cost-plus or target-return basis.	❏	❏	❏	❏	❏	❏	❏	We set prices based on customer value.
2. CREDIT EXTENSION Our credit policy is rigidly applied regardless of customer.	❏	❏	❏	❏	❏	❏	❏	Our credit policy is informed by the strategic realities we face.

G. BUSINESS ORGANIZATION

	1	2	3	4	5	6	7	
1. APPROACH TO STRUCTURE Our organizational structure is characterized by functional silos.	❏	❏	❏	❏	❏	❏	❏	We place high value on cross-functional integration.

B. THE FIRM/BUSINESS UNIT'S APPROACH TO MARKETING

Use Figure 1B.1 to develop a *map* that assesses the firm/business unit's approach to marketing. Focus on the business unit rather than the entire firm for an existing product/service, or on your proposed organization for a startup.

- Review your scale scores. Write a paragraph that assesses the way your business organization approaches marketing.

- From what you know right now, which three marketing imperatives will be most important to your marketing case? Why? Insert your response in Figure 1B.2.

- From what you know right now, which two marketing principles will have most application to your marketing case? Insert your response in Figure 1B.2.

FIGURE 1B.1

THE FIRM/BUSINESS UNIT'S APPROACH TO MARKETING

In this organization, the perspective taken by senior management is that:

	1	2	3	4	5	6	7	
Organizational survival is the major firm objective.	❑	❑	❑	❑	❑	❑	❑	Shareholder value is the major firm objective.
Accounting profit is critical.	❑	❑	❑	❑	❑	❑	❑	Shareholder value is critical.
Product markets are pre-eminent.	❑	❑	❑	❑	❑	❑	❑	Capital markets are pre-eminent.
Marketing is one of the functions.	❑	❑	❑	❑	❑	❑	❑	Marketing is a philosophy as well as a function.
We manage the *status quo*.	❑	❑	❑	❑	❑	❑	❑	We manage change.
Customers are a necessary evil.	❑	❑	❑	❑	❑	❑	❑	Customers are key assets.
The supplier chooses options.	❑	❑	❑	❑	❑	❑	❑	The customer chooses options.
Seller power dominates.	❑	❑	❑	❑	❑	❑	❑	Customer power dominates.
Customers have non-discretionary purchasing power.	❑	❑	❑	❑	❑	❑	❑	Customers have discretionary purchasing power.
The firm accepts all orders.	❑	❑	❑	❑	❑	❑	❑	The firm selects customers.
A department markets.	❑	❑	❑	❑	❑	❑	❑	The business-unit/firm markets.
Marketing is a one-way process.	❑	❑	❑	❑	❑	❑	❑	Marketing is an interactive process.

FIGURE 1B.2

IMPORTANCE OF MARKETING IMPERATIVES AND MARKETING PRINCIPLES

MARKETING IMPERATIVES	REASON FOR IMPORTANCE
MARKETING PRINCIPLES	**REASON FOR IMPORTANCE**

CHAPTER 2: THE VALUE OF CUSTOMERS

In this chapter you estimate the lifetime value (CLV) for a current or potential customer in the market arena you are considering. You may have several choices for customer type: you could select a consumer or an entity within the distribution channel. You may wish to consider more than one customer type. Regardless, clearly specify your focal customer.

A. DETERMINATION OF CUSTOMER LIFETIME VALUE (CLV): CURRENT CUSTOMERS

Think about the customers for your product/service. Make an estimate of current customer lifetime value by entering data in Figure 2A.1 and performing the related calculations. If you are in a B2C business, you may select a consumer as an exemplar of a particular market segment. If you are in B2B, you may select an individual customer. If your firm/business unit has no current customers, or if you prefer to focus on potential customers, do a similar analysis, but be sure to include a term for *acquisition cost*.

Complete the following steps in Figure 2A.1:

1. Calculate **net profit margin (m)** from sales revenues and costs.
2. Determine **annual maintenance expense (a)** per customer.
3. Calculate **adjusted profit margin (m − a)**, by taking the net profit margin (m) and subtracting the annual maintenance expense (a).
4. Determine firm **discount rate (d)**[*].
5. Determine year-to-year **customer retention rate (r)** (or *customer retention probability* for an individual customer).
6. Calculate **margin multiple — $r/(1 + d − r)$**.
7. Calculate **CLV** by multiplying the adjusted profit margin by the margin multiple.

FIGURE 2A.1:

CUSTOMER LIFETIME VALUE (CLV) CALCULATION

	Term	Calculation	Value
1	Net profit margin	m	
2	Annual maintenance expense	a	
3	Adjusted profit margin	m − a	
4	Discount rate	d	
5	Customer retention rate	r	
6	Margin multiple	$r/(1 + d − r)$	
7	Customer lifetime value (CLV)	$(m − a) \times r/(1 + d − r)$	

8. How do you assess the results of your **CLV** calculation? Does the figure you calculated make sense? What are the implications for the firm/business unit? What options will you consider in addressing selected customers?

B. CUSTOMER RELATIONSHIP MANAGEMENT

In Figure 2B.1, you explore your firm/business unit's efforts at customer relationship management (CRM). To be able to complete this exercise you will need access to knowledgeable executives.

- What CRM programs does your firm/business unit have in place?
- How do you assess the success of these programs?
- What suggestions do you have for improving your CRM efforts?

---

[*]The appropriate discount rate is the firm's cost of capital; see any good introductory finance text.

FIGURE 2B.1

CUSTOMER
RELATIONSHIP
MANAGEMENT
(CRM)

CRM Programs in Place	Assessment of CRM Programs	Suggestions for Improvement

Managing Marketing in the 21st Century

SECTION I: MARKETING AND THE FIRM

CHAPTER 1
Introduction to Managing Marketing

CHAPTER 2
The Value of Customers

SECTION II: FUNDAMENTAL INSIGHTS FOR STRATEGIC MARKETING

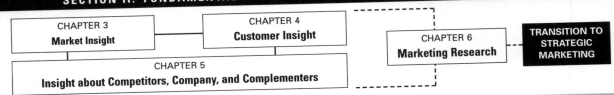

CHAPTER 3
Market Insight

CHAPTER 4
Customer Insight

CHAPTER 6
Marketing Research

TRANSITION TO STRATEGIC MARKETING

CHAPTER 5
Insight about Competitors, Company, and Complementers

SECTION III: STRATEGIC MARKETING

IMPERATIVE 1
Determine and Recommend Which Markets to Address

CHAPTER 7
Identifying and Choosing Opportunities

IMPERATIVE 2
Identify and Target Market Segments

CHAPTER 8
Market Segmentation and Targeting

IMPERATIVE 3
Set Strategic Direction and Positioning

CHAPTER 9
Market Strategy: Integrating Firm Efforts for Marketing Success

CHAPTER 10
Managing through the Life Cycle

CHAPTER 11
Managing Brands

SECTION IV: IMPLEMENTING THE MARKET STRATEGY

IMPERATIVE 4
Design the Market Offer

PART A: PROVIDING CUSTOMER VALUE

PART B: COMMUNICATING CUSTOMER VALUE

PART C: DELIVERING CUSTOMER VALUE

PART D: GETTING PAID FOR CUSTOMER VALUE

CHAPTER 12
Managing the Product Line

CHAPTER 15
Integrated Marketing Communications

CHAPTER 18
Distribution Decisions

CHAPTER 19
Critical Underpinnings of Pricing Decisions

CHAPTER 13
Managing Services and Customer Service

CHAPTER 16
Mass and Digital Communication

CHAPTER 20
Setting Prices

CHAPTER 14
Developing New Products

CHAPTER 17
Directing and Managing the Field Sales Effort

IMPERATIVE 5
Secure Support from Other Functions

CHAPTER 21
Ensuring the Firm Implements the Market Offer as Planned

IMPERATIVE 6
Monitor and Control

CHAPTER 22
Monitoring and Controlling Firm Functioning and Performance

SECTION V: SPECIAL MARKETING TOPICS

CHAPTER 23
International, Regional, and Global Marketing

Section II: Fundamental Insights for Strategic Marketing

CHAPTER 3: MARKET INSIGHT

In this chapter you complete a sequence of exercises designed to provide greater insight into the market for your chosen product/service.

A. MARKET STRUCTURE ANALYSIS

The purpose of this exercise is to provide a process allowing you to think more broadly about the market for your product/service. This way, you will not miss opportunities that are in some way related to the current market offer. Figure 3A.1 provides an example.

FIGURE 3A.1

MARKET STRUCTURE FOR TREATING ANEURYSMS

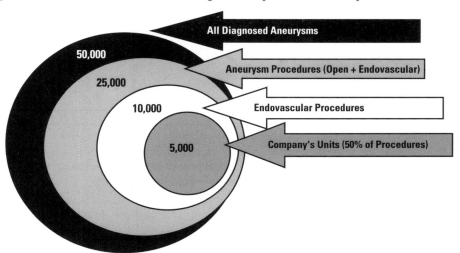

In Figure 3A.2, identify your market structure. Remember to start with the broadest possible definition of the market, then get narrower, and eventually focus on the firm/business unit's products. What are the implications of the market structure for your firm/business unit?

FIGURE 3A.2

MARKET STRUCTURE ANALYSIS

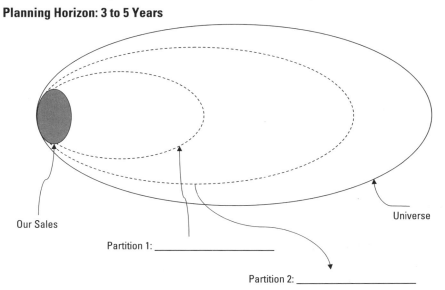

B. PRODUCT EVOLUTION

Your current product/service is one entry in a product form; the product form is one of several forms in a broader product class. As you learned in the text, *product-class life cycles* and *product-form life cycles* are each shorter than the market life cycle. Furthermore, these product forms and product classes evolve over time — Figure 3B.1.

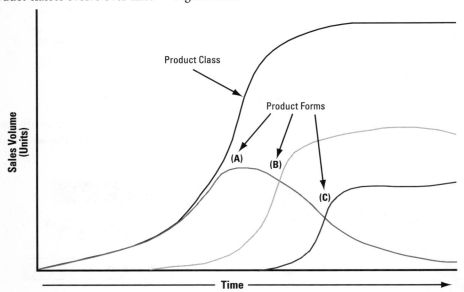

FIGURE 3B.1

PRODUCT-CLASS AND PRODUCT-FORM LIFE CYCLES

In Figure 3B.2, plot the trajectory of the product class and the various product forms in the product class. Start from several years ago and project several years into the future. What are the implications of the product life-cycle analysis for your firm/business unit?

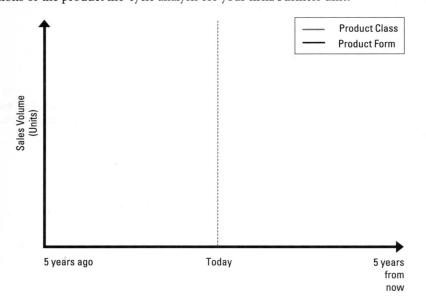

FIGURE 3B.2

PRODUCT LIFE-CYCLE ANALYSIS

C. INDUSTRY FORCES

Your firm/business unit faces several important forces in its industry environment. We adopt the **five-forces model** comprising current direct competitors, new direct entrants, indirect competitors, suppliers, and buyers. In Figure 3C.1, identify the important players in each area and isolate the potential impact of each player.

FIGURE 3C.1

INDUSTRY FORCES ANALYSIS

Planning Horizon: 3 to 5 Years

Industry Force	Important Players	Potential Impact on the Firm/Business Unit
Current direct competitors		
New direct competitors		
Indirect competitors		
Suppliers		
Buyers		

D. ENVIRONMENTAL FORCES

In addition to industry forces that directly affect the firm, managers must also consider a set of environmental forces impacting both the firm/business unit and the various industry forces. These **PESTLE** forces include **p**olitical, **e**conomic, **s**ociocultural, **t**echnological, **l**egal, and **e**nvironmental (physical).

- In Figure 3D.1, identify important exemplars of these forces you expect to impact your firm/ business unit (and the various industry players) over the next three to five years. (For example, potential economic exemplars may include interest rates, exchange rates, and inflation.) Identify the potential impact of these forces on your firm/ business unit.

FIGURE 3D.1

ENVIRONMENTAL FORCES ANALYSIS

Planning Horizon: 3 to 5 Years

Force	Important Exemplars	Potential Impact on the Firm/Business Unit
Political		
Economic		
Sociocultural		
Technological		
Legal		
Environment (Physical)		

- In Figure 3D.2, summarize each environmental force and its effect. (Think of a newspaper headline.)

Planning Horizon: 3 to 5 Years

Force	Summary of Impact of Environmental Force
Political	
Economic	
Sociocultural	
Technological	
Legal	
Environment (Physical)	

- In Figure 3D.3, identify the major challenges and opportunities for your firm/business unit based on the **PESTLE** forces analysis.

Planning Horizon: 3 to 5 Years

Challenges for the Firm/Business Unit

Opportunities for the Firm/Business Unit

E. MARKET INSIGHT

Based on results of the previous exercises, what insight have you gained about the market your firm/business unit is facing? What issues most concern you? Use Figure 3E.1.

FIGURE 3E.1

MARKET INSIGHT SUMMARY

Planning Horizon: 3 to 5 Years

Key Insights for the Firm/Business Unit
Major Issues the Firm/Business Unit Must Address

CHAPTER 4: CUSTOMER INSIGHT

In this chapter, we focus on gaining insight into those customers in the market arena for your product/service. We focus on six specific areas:

A. Macro-level customers

B. The purchase-decision process

C. Roles of individuals in the purchase-decision process

D. Benefits and values for customers

E. The attributes/benefits/values ladder

F. Economic value for the customer

A. MACRO-LEVEL CUSTOMERS

Who are the macro-level customers? We address this question by means of the purchase-decision map in Figure 4A.1. This template provides several spaces to identify different sorts of entities at the macro level. We can view each of these entities as a form of customer. Customer types include:

- **Direct customers** for the product/service.
- **Customers of the direct customer** that may purchase the product/service from direct customers. These indirect customers may include manufacturers, distributors, jobbers, manufacturers' representatives, retailers, or consumers. Note there may be several organization types.
- **Customers of the direct customers' customers** may include similar entities to those noted in the previous bullet point.
- **End users** for the product/service.
- Other **firm business units** that may purchase the product/service or otherwise be involved in the purchase decision.
- **Third-party influencer/advisor organizations** that may influence the purchase decision.

Use Figure 4A.1 to complete the purchase-decision map. Note: You may need to add more customer types. Alternatively, some entries in the figure may not apply to your situation — for example, retailers if your firm/business unit focuses on B2B markets.

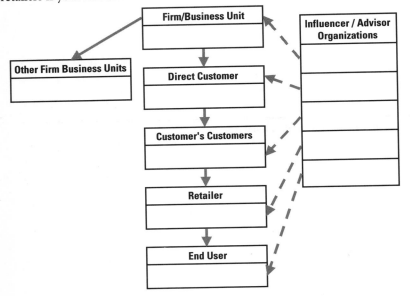

FIGURE 4A.1

PURCHASE-
DECISION MAP

B. PURCHASE-DECISION PROCESS

In part A, you just identified various *customers* in the purchase decision. Now let's identify the most important customer type for the purchase decision and walk through their buying process. Answer the questions posed in Figure 4B.1. What insight did you gain about the purchase-decision process for this customer type? How should the firm/business unit think about modifying its actions? We highly recommend that you supplement secondary data with one or more customer DILOs — *day in the life of*. There is nothing like talking to real customers to gain insight.

When you complete this analysis for the most important customer type, repeat the process for other important customer types.

Purchase-Decision Step	Questions to Ask	Behavior of Customer Type
Recognizing problems	How do these customers recognize the problem that a purchase will solve? Are there specific "triggers" that raise customer awareness?	
Acquiring information	What sorts of information do these customers seek?	
Evaluating alternatives	How do these customers evaluate alternatives?	
Making a choice	What choices are these customers likely to make?	
Post-purchase processes	What sorts of decisions do these customers make after purchase?	

FIGURE 4B.1

PURCHASE-
DECISION PROCESS

C. ROLES IN THE PURCHASE-DECISION PROCESS

For each important macro-level customer type you identified in Step A, complete the Roles Map Template — Figure 4C.1. For each person involved in the purchase decision, identify their role, organizational position, and degree of influence on the purchase process; their perception of the firm/business unit and its competitors as suppliers; their relationships with the firm/business unit and its competitors; the person's own reputation; items important to the person; and their *hot buttons*.

Recall from your textbook that possible roles are specifier, gatekeeper, buyer, coach, decision-maker, gatekeeper, influencer (champion/sponsor, spoiler), information provider, initiator, specifier, and user.

FIGURE 4C.1

ROLES IN THE PURCHASE-DECISION PROCESS

Name	Role in the Decision Process	Organization Position/Degree of Influence	Perceptions of Our Firm/ Business Unit versus Competitors	Our Firm/ Business Unit's Relationships versus Competitors'	Reputation/ Personal Interests	"Hot Buttons"

Of course, many purchase decisions are made not by individuals but by groups of individuals acting together. Sometimes these individuals have similar goals regarding the purchase; sometimes their goals are quite disparate. Use Figure 4C.2 to examine the nature of group decision-making for the purchase about which you are most concerned.

Question	Response
Will the purchase decision be made by an individual or by a group? If a group, who do you expect to be involved?	
What are the power relationships among purchase-decision actors?	
Do you expect coalitions of individuals to form for this purchase decision? If yes, identify the coalitions.	
What mechanisms does the customer use to resolve purchase-decision conflicts?	
Based on your answers to the foregoing questions, what actions should you consider taking?	

FIGURE 4C.2

MULTIPLE-PERSON PURCHASE-DECISION PROCESS

D. BENEFITS AND VALUES FOR CUSTOMERS

The firm/business unit builds products/services with features and attributes — customers seek benefits and values. In this exercise, you identify benefits and values for each of the important macro-level customer types. For the most important customer type:

- Brainstorm the benefits and values required (needs to be satisfied) in general by customers in the market. These benefits (needs) may be functional, psychological, or economic. Do not pause to discuss any item or worry about potential overlaps. Benefits (needs) will likely be of the form:
  - no down time
  - low risk of defective product
  - excellent taste
  - ease of manufacture for customer's product

Do not focus on the features/attributes your firm/business unit offers. For example, comparable features (benefits) may be:
  - on-time delivery (no down time)
  - high levels of quality control (low risk of defective product)
  - high quality ingredients (excellent taste)
  - high quality product design (ease of manufacture of customer's product).

Rather, focus on those benefits that you believe customers desire. Use Figure 4D.1 to brainstorm a list of benefits and values.

- When you have finished brainstorming, reduce your list of benefits/values to six to eight items. Do this by regrouping to place related benefits (needs) into a single category. Feel free to reorder your benefits/values. Write your benefit/value set on Figure 4D.2.

- Be sure to save the benefit/value set. These benefits/values are important input for Exercise A in the Market Segmentation analysis — Chapter 8.

FIGURE 4D.1

BRAINSTORMING REQUIRED CUSTOMER BENEFITS (NEEDS)

1. _____   8. _____

2. _____   9. _____

3. _____   10. _____

4. _____   11. _____

5. _____   12. _____

6. _____   13. _____

7. _____   14. _____

FIGURE 4D.2

CONSOLIDATED REQUIRED CUSTOMER BENEFITS (NEEDS) LIST

1. _____   5. _____

2. _____   6. _____

3. _____   7. _____

4. _____   8. _____

Repeat this and subsequent analyses for other important customer types.

E. THE FEATURES/BENEFITS/VALUES LADDER

We designed the features/benefits/value ladder to encourage you to think more deeply about customer benefits/values than in the previous exercise. While completing this exercise, feel free to use the benefits and values that you identified in Figure 4D.1, but do not be constrained by them. Use the chart in Figure 4E.1 to develop the features/benefits/values ladder for your product for each important customer type. You secure greater insight if you address this issue in two different ways. For your product:

1. MOVE UP THE LADDER

- Identify the features/attributes of the product/service ("how" it is constructed).
- Identify the benefits customers receive from these features/attributes. Note there may be different levels of benefits ("what" it does).
- Identify the values these benefits deliver to customers ("why" they are important to the customer).

2. MOVE DOWN THE LADDER

- Identify values the firm/business unit may deliver to customer.
- Identify benefits the firm/business unit may deliver that could give rise to these values.
- Identify the features/attributes the firm/business unit would require to deliver these benefits.

	Start from Features/Attributes and work up the ladder	Start from Values and work down the ladder
Customer Values		
Benefit Level 3		
Benefit Level 2		
Benefit Level 1		
Features/Attributes		

FIGURE 4E.1

THE FEATURES/
BENEFITS/VALUES
LADDER

3. EXAMINE THE BENEFITS AND VALUES YOU IDENTIFIED.

- Think about customer needs — are you missing any important benefits/values?
- Are the benefits/values you identified dominated by economic and functional items? If so, are there more psychological benefits/values you could identify?
- What additional insight did you secure from completing the ladders from the two directions?
- Did the different ways of approaching the ladders give you different results?
- Finally, do the benefits and values you identified satisfy important customer needs?

Repeat this analysis for other important customer types.

The results of this analysis are important inputs into Exercise A in the Market Segmentation analysis — Chapter 8.

F. ECONOMIC VALUE FOR THE CUSTOMER

Complete this section if your product offers economic value to customers. We discuss economic value for the customer (EVC) in your textbook — Chapter 4; we revisit the concept in Chapter 19 because it is integral to many pricing decisions. Figure 4F.1 demonstrates the economic value the firm/business unit delivers. Note there are four critical concepts:

- **Reference value** — the price of the most directly competitive product
- **Positive differentiation value** — the positive economic values the firm/business unit's product adds
- **Negative differentiation value** — the costs (negative economic values) the customer incurs from using the firm/business unit's product
- **Total economic value** — the net of the reference value plus the positive differentiation value, less the negative differentiation value

FIGURE 4F.1

ECONOMIC VALUE
FOR THE CUSTOMER

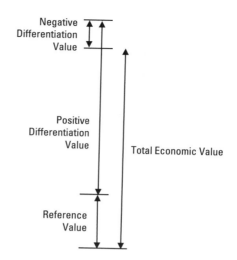

To calculate total economic value, the firm must complete several steps:

- Identify the most directly competitive product and assess its price.
- Identify the sources of positive economic value for the customer — Figure 4F.2.
- Identify the sources of additional costs (negative economic value) for the customer — Figure 4F.2.
- Estimate the value these sources provide — Figure 4F.3.
- Estimate the costs attributable to these sources — Figure 4F.3.
- Calculate the total economic value the firm's product provides — Figure 4F.4.

FIGURE 4F.2

BRAINSTORM SOURCES
OF POSITIVE ECONOMIC
VALUE AND ADDITIONAL
COSTS FOR THE
CUSTOMER

Sources of Positive Economic Value	Sources of Additional Costs

Sources of Positive Economic Value	Economic Value ($)	Sources of Additional Costs	Additional Costs ($)
Total		**•Total**	

FIGURE 4F.3

ECONOMIC VALUE TABLE

Reference Value – Price of Competitive Product	
Total of Positive Sources of Economic Value	
Sum of Refence Value plus Positive Sources	
Total Additional Costs	
Total Economic Value	

FIGURE 4F.4

CALCULATION OF ECONOMIC VALUE

CHAPTER 5: INSIGHT ABOUT COMPETITORS, COMPANY, AND COMPLEMENTERS

In Chapter 5, we complete several exercises designed to provide insight into competitors and complementers. In this chapter, you complete six exercises designed to provide insight into competition the firm/business unit faces:

A. Identifying Competitors and Complementers

B. Value-Chain Analysis

C. SWOT Analysis

D. Competitor Assessment Analysis

E. Competitor Strategy Analysis

F. Complementer Analysis

A. IDENTIFYING COMPETITORS AND COMPLEMENTERS

In the *Industry Analysis* — Chapter 3 — we identified several types of competitor. In this exercise, we revisit competitor identification and also identify complementers. We use Figure 5A.1 to identify competitors and complementers. The figure has two dimensions: the vertical axis identifies whether the competitor is active today (*current*) or may be a competitor tomorrow (*potential*). The horizontal axis captures the extent to which the type of competition is *direct* or *indirect* — the figure allows for different levels of directness and indirectness of competition. On the right-hand side of the figure is space for complementers.

Note that you may want to think about the competitor at two different levels. For example, at one level, Eli Lilly offers Cialis for erectile dysfunction, competing with Viagra. At another level, Eli Lilly competes with Pfizer overall. If a much smaller and less successful firm offered a Viagra substitute, Pfizer would face a very different type and level of competition.

FIGURE 5A.1

IDENTIFYING COMPETITORS AND COMPLEMENTERS

Competitors
Direct | Indirect

Complementers

Actual

Potential

Identify three competitors the firm/business unit should be most concerned about:

1.
2.
3.

- **Competitors: current position.** Identify the current position of your competitors — direct and indirect, current (today) and potential (tomorrow), and your complementers. Be sure to identify both the competitive (complementer) brand and competitive (complementer) firm.

- **Competitors: future position.** Project the future position of your competitors and complementers over a three-to-five-year time horizon — use an arrow to indicate their likely new location (cell) on the chart. For example, some current competitors and/or complementers will leave the market; some potential competitors and/or complementers may enter the market. (Refer to *MM21C* — Figure 5.5; *CMF* — Figure 5.4.)

- **Competitors: main threats.** Based on the figure, what insights do you have about the future competitive landscape? Determine which three competitors are the most serious threats to the firm/business unit.

- **Competitors: level.** For the three competitors you chose, on what level of the competitor's organization will you focus your analysis (e.g., corporate, business unit, or product)? What additional information would you like to improve your analysis? What types of internal or external sources could be helpful to you? (Refer to *MM21C* — Table 5.2; *CMF* — Table 5.1.)

- **Complementers: assessment.** How do you assess the current and future situation as regards complementers?

B. VALUE-CHAIN ANALYSIS

We use the value-chain analysis from Chapter 7 to gain insight into individual competitors. Figure 5B.1 shows a generic value chain. We use the value-chain concept to deconstruct each of the chosen three competitors — Figure 5B.2.

FIGURE 5B.1

A GENERIC BUSINESS

Research and Development › Product Design › Manufacturing › Marketing › Physical Distribution › Sales › Service

ACTIVITY							
Cost Advantage							
Value Advantage							

Major Strengths and Example	
Major Weaknesses and Example	

The essence of value-chain analysis is to compare the competitor against the firm/business unit by means of a differential diagnosis. We use the value chain in Figure 5B.2 to conduct this diagnosis:

- Describe the competitor value chain using the chevrons in the figure. You are not restricted to the number of chevrons in the figure; use more or fewer as needed.
- For each stage, identify where the competitor has a:
  - Cost advantage
  - Value advantage
- Based on your analysis, what competitor capabilities/resources constitute its:
  - Major strengths
  - Major weaknesses
- Give a concrete example of where the competitor has deployed its strengths.
- Give a concrete example of where the competitor has faced difficulties because of its weaknesses.

Use the same templates for competitors 2 and 3.

C. SWOT ANALYSIS

The SWOT analysis builds on the value-chain analysis. In this analysis, you identify your firm/business unit's strengths and weaknesses versus specific competitors — in particular, those competitors you identified in section 5A. You also identify opportunities and threats. Using the results of your analysis in Figure 5B.1, complete Figure 5C.1:

- Assess your firm/business unit's *strengths* relative to each competitor. What do you do better than your competitors? How are your products/services superior?

- Assess your firm/business unit's *weaknesses* relative to each competitor. What do your competitors do better than you? How are your products/services weaker? What organizational issues or roadblocks have contributed to the weaker position?

- Based on your firm/business unit's strengths and weaknesses, what *opportunities* are available to your firm/business unit? In other words, where may you find additional business?

- Based on your firm/business unit's strengths and weaknesses, what *threats* and/or challenges does your firm/business unit face? How badly could those threats damage its performance?

- What additional information would you require to improve your analysis?

FIGURE 5C.1

SWOT ANALYSIS

Strengths	Weaknesses
Opportunities	**Threats**

Key items of competitor information required for a deeper analysis:

1.
2.
3.

D. COMPETITOR ASSESSMENT ANALYSIS

This analysis offers a deeper view of how the firm/business unit stacks up against competitors. The analysis seeks understanding where the firm/business unit has a differential advantage over competitors. Recall that the firm has a differential advantage when it provides a net benefit, or cluster of benefits, to a sizeable group of customers, that they value and are willing to pay for, but cannot get, or believe they cannot get, elsewhere.

For this analysis, use Figure 5D.1. For the product and the market that is the focus of this analysis:

- From Chapter 4 – Customer Insight. Identify the **benefits/values** sought by customers. See in particular Sections 4D and 4E. Place these benefits/values in priority order beginning with the most important and enter them into the left-hand column of the figure. In the adjacent column, insert the importance rank for customers.

- For each **benefit/value**, identify the *organizational capabilities/resources* any firm would require to provide customers with these benefits.values. These capabilities/resources may include:
  - Deep pockets (for funding R&D)
  - Multiple distribution points (for on-time delivery)

- Low cost manufacturing (for low prices)
- Excellent customer service (for high customer retention)

These capabilities/resources should represent the ideal; whether or not your firm/business unit possesses them is not the issue. Brainstorming may help you generate a suitable list of capabilities/resources.

Enter these capabilities/resources in the top row of the figure.

- **Identify the matches.** Mark with an asterisk (*) those matrix cells where a particular organizational capability/resource would be required to deliver a customer benefit/value. If there is no relationship, leave the cell blank. (Most likely these markings will occur in only a fraction of the possible intersections.)

- For each cell marked with an asterisk, compare your firm/business unit to its competitors and ask up to three questions[3]:

  - **Relevance.** Does your firm/business unit possess the necessary capabilities/resources?
    - **Y** There is a good match between the benefit/value customers require and your firm/business unit's ability to supply.
    - **N** There is a mismatch. Your firm/business unit lacks the capabilities/resources required to provide the benefit/value.

  - **Superiority.** For those cells where you placed a **Y** for the relevance question, how does your firm/business unit compare with competitors?
    - **Y** Your firm/business unit possesses these capabilities/resources to a superior degree, far better than competitors.
    - **N** As regards these capabilities/resources, your firm/business unit rates no better than competitors.

  - **Sustainability.** For those cells where you placed a **Y** for the superiority question, how easy would it be for competitors to acquire/develop your capabilities/resources?
    - **Y** It would be very difficult for competitors to acquire/develop these capabilities/resources, given the costs and/or time required.
    - **N** Parity in this area could be achieved fairly easily.

  Each cell with an asterisk will contain one of the following entries — **N, YN, YYN,** or **YYY.**

- For each customer benefit/value, summarize the results of your analysis for each relevant organizational capability/resource — Figure 5D.2

- Summarize the overall results of your analysis, also in Figure 5D.2:
  - What do you know about your firm/business unit's competitive position regarding customer benefits/values that you did not know before completing this analysis?
  - Where does your firm/business unit possess a sustainable differential advantage — **YYY?**
  - What actions should your firm/business unit contemplate to sustain a differential advantage?
  - Where does your firm/business unit have an advantage that is not sustainable — **YYN?**
  - How might you turn this advantage into a *sustainable* differential advantage?
  - If you do not have a differential advantage — **YN,** what actions could your firm/business unit take to secure one?
  - Where do your competitors have differential advantages — **N?**

- What additional information would you require to improve your analysis?

FIGURE 5D.1

COMPETITOR
ASSESSMENT
ANALYSIS

Required Capabilities/Resources

Customer Required Benefits/ Values	Importance Rank							

FIGURE 5D.2

COMPETITOR
ASSESSMENT
ANALYSIS –
SUMMARY

Customer Required Benefits/Values	Summarize Results per Required Benefits/Value	Potential Sources of Firm/Business Unit Differential Advantages	Potential Sources of Competitor Differential Advantages

Key items of competitor information required for a deeper analysis:

1.

2.

3.

E. COMPETITOR STRATEGY ANALYSIS

This analysis attempts to identify competitors' likely strategy, to assess how big a threat an individual competitor is to the firm/business unit, and to develop some ideas of how the firm/business unit may consider responding. Use Figure 5E.1 to answer the following questions about the firm/business unit's competitors:

a. Based on the previous exercises, identify each competitor that poses a significant threat to the firm/business unit.

b. For each competitor you identified in (a), determine its market share.

c. For each competitor, assess the level of threat according to the following scheme:
   • **Dominant** — dictates strategies of other firms
   • **Strong** — can act independent of others without damaging itself

- **Favorable** — has unique strength, can potentially improve position
- **Tenable** — will continue to participate, unlikely to improve position
- **Weak** — poor position, continued participation in question

d. Based on the competitor's observed actions, assess its objectives. For example, the competitor may hope to:

- Increase market share
- Hold market share
- Increase profits
- Hold profits at current level
- Increase cash flow
- Continue same cash flow
- Drive competitors out of the market
- Plan a market exit

e. Based on your assessment of competitor objectives in (d), what strategy do you expect the competitor to adopt?

f. Identify some potential responses that your firm/business unit could take to address competitor strategy.

g. What additional information would you require to improve your analysis?

Competitor	Market Share	Level of Competitor Threat to the Firm/ Business Unit	Likely Competitor Objectives	Likely Competitor Strategy	Possible Firm/ Business Unit Strategy

FIGURE 5E.1

COMPETITOR STRATEGY ANALYSIS

Key items of competitor information required for a deeper analysis:

1.

2.

3.

F. COMPLEMENTER ANALYSIS

The purpose of this analysis is to investigate more deeply the complementers you identified in 5A.1 – Identifying Competitors and Complementers. Use Figure 5F.1 to answer the following questions about firm/business unit complementers:

- Identify the firm/business unit's three most important complementers.
- For each complementer you identified:
  - What is the nature of the complementarity?
  - Is the complementer likely to become more or less important to the firm/business unit? Why? Or why not?
  - What actions is the complementer likely to take that will affect the firm/business unit?
  - What actions should the firm/business unit consider to gain maximum benefit from the complementer?
  - What else would you like to know about the complementer?

FIGURE 5F.1

COMPLEMENTER
ANALYSIS

Complementer	Nature of Complementarity	Likelihood of Change in Complementer Importance to the Firm/Business Unit	Likely Complementer Actions That will Impact the Firm/ Business Unit	Possible Firm Actions

What else would you like to know about complementers?

1.

2.

3.

CHAPTER 6: MARKETING RESEARCH

We focus on potentials and forecasts. By completing the exercises in Chapters 3, 4, and 5, we hope you have gained significant market; customer; and competitor, firm, and complementer insight. This insight is essential in allowing you to develop a set of planning assumptions about the market; customers; and competitors, firm, and complementers the firm/business unit faces.

A. ESTIMATING MARKET POTENTIAL

In Figure 3A.2 — Chapter 3 — you developed the market structure, by identifying several market partitions. Using that structure and Figure 6A.1, make an estimate of market potential for a three- or five-year time horizon.

FIGURE 6A.1

MARKET POTENTIAL
ESTIMATE (UNITS
OR DOLLARS)

Market Partition	Total Number of Customers A	Percent Likely to Buy (%) B	Number of Customers Likely to Buy C = A x B	Number of Units (dollars) That Those Purchasing Are Likely to Buy D	Market Partition Potential Calculation E = C x D
1.					
2.					
3.					
				Total Market Potential (Units or Dollars)	

B. FORECASTING MARKET SIZE

In your marketing textbook, we presented several methods for forecasting market size. We identified two judgmental approaches — executive judgment and the Delphi method; four time-based methods — judgmental extrapolation, linear extrapolation, moving average, and exponential smoothing; and one causal factor method — multiple regression.

Select a method, and forecast market size for each year in your planning horizon, say for five years. Now choose a second method and make another forecast independently. Assess the consistency of your forecasts, explain the discrepancies, and decide what forecasts you will work with — Figure 6B.1.

Forecasting Method	Year 1	Year 2	Year 3	Year 4	Year 5
1					
2					
Working Forecast					

FIGURE 6B.1

FORECASTING MARKET SIZE (UNITS OR DOLLARS)

C. SALES FORECAST

Forecasting your firm/business unit's sales in the various years is now simply a matter of taking market size forecasts from Figure 6B.1 and multiplying by market share estimates. Make these estimates and calculations in Figure 6C.1. Develop both unit and dollar forecasts. If your market potential and market size forecasts were in units, make sales revenue forecasts by estimating your firm/business unit's average selling price. Use the figure to justify your market share estimates.

	Year 1	Year 2	Year 3	Year 4	Year 5
Market Forecast (from Figure 6B.1)					
Market Share Estimate					
Justification of Market Share Estimate					
Sales Forecast (units)					
Forecast Average Selling Price					
Sales Forecast (dollars)					

FIGURE 6C.1

FORECASTING THE FIRM/BUSINESS UNIT'S SALES (UNITS OR DOLLARS)

TRANSITION TO STRATEGIC MARKETING

A. PLANNING ASSUMPTIONS

Planning assumptions help us to:

- Anticipate the future and identify forces for change
- Outline the business conditions under which we expect to operate
- Build the foundation for the strategic marketing plan
- Build *trip wires* to identify unforeseen changes

Recall that *planning assumptions* are the set of conditions, over which we have no control, that are critical to market attractiveness. Mostly, planning assumptions are about matters external to the firm/business unit. For example:

- The market for textiles will grow at more than 3.5 percent annually.
- Asian brands will continue to gain at least 10 percent market share.
- New local chemical suppliers will gain at least 8 percent share.
- E-commerce will capture more than 15 percent of revenues for textile chemicals.
- New fibers will be introduced and gain more than 10 percent market share.
- Environmental regulations will increase costs significantly or cause major chemicals to be removed from production processes.
- Consumers will not accept price increases greater than 1 percent per annum.
- Two of our chemical suppliers will integrate forward and capture 10 percent market share.

Regardless, some planning assumptions may be internal to the firm/business unit:

- Our new plant will come on stream in January 20XY.
- Our new product will be ready for launch in July 20XZ.

In this transition we address several related exercises to build robust planning assumptions:

- Using Figure T.1, brainstorm a set of planning assumptions for the next three to five years.
- Using Figure T.2, cull the list of assumptions from Figure T.1 and assess the probability of each assumption occurring and its likely impact were it to occur or not occur.
- Plot each assumption from Figure T.2 in Figure T.3.
- Identify the most critical planning assumptions — those in the upper-right corner of the chart and indicate whether or not you are able to influence the assumption. Use **L** to indicate low chance, **M** for moderate chance, and **H** for high chance.
- For each critical planning assumption, using Figure T.4, develop a "We believe ..." statement and the corresponding implications for your firm/business unit. For example:

    "*We believe* that market growth will exceed 10 percent annually."

    Implication: We shall have to increase production capacity and broaden distribution to maintain market share.

- For any assumption about which there is significant uncertainty, consider the following options:

    - Can you gather additional information to reduce the uncertainty?
    - If you cannot gain additional information, are there only a few alternatives that may occur? If so, you should state these and be prepared to develop contingency strategies at a later stage.

- If you identify multiple alternatives, you should be prepared to conduct extensive scenario analyses of possible options so you can identify a robust strategy — a strategy that will be successful regardless of eventual competitive actions.
- Use Figure T.5 to capture the results of your analysis.

1._____   8._____

2._____   9._____

3._____   10._____

4._____   11._____

5._____   12._____

6._____   13._____

7._____   14._____

FIGURE T.1

BRAINSTORM PLANNING ASSUMPTIONS

Assumption	Probability of Occurrence	Magnitude of Effect
1.		
2.		
3.		
4.		
5.		
6.		
7.		
8.		
9.		
10.		

FIGURE T.2

CULL ASSUMPTIONS – IDENTIFY MAGNITUDE OF EFFECT AND PROBABILITY OF OCCURRENCE

FIGURE T.3

PLOT PLANNING ASSUMPTIONS

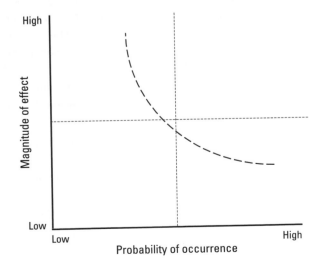

FIGURE T.4

"WE BELIEVE ..."
STATEMENTS AND
IMPLICATIONS
FOR PLANNING
ASSUMPTIONS
ABOUT WHICH
WE ARE CONFIDENT

"We believe…"	Implications

FIGURE T.5

ACTION IMPLICATIONS
FOR PLANNING
ASSUMPTIONS ABOUT
WHICH WE ARE
QUITE UNCERTAIN

Uncertain Assumptions	Information about the Assumptions	Contingency Plan and Specific Contingencies	Possible Scenarios

ANALYSIS CHECK

You must make sure that your recommendations are supported by your earlier analyses. Go back to your analyses in the previous chapters — especially Chapters 3, 4, 5, and 6 — and make sure that they support your planning assumptions.

Managing Marketing in the 21ˢᵗ Century

SECTION I: MARKETING AND THE FIRM

CHAPTER 1
Introduction to Managing Marketing

CHAPTER 2
The Value of Customers

SECTION II: FUNDAMENTAL INSIGHTS FOR STRATEGIC MARKETING

CHAPTER 3
Market Insight

CHAPTER 4
Customer Insight

CHAPTER 5
Insight about Competitors, Company, and Complementers

CHAPTER 6
Marketing Research

TRANSITION TO STRATEGIC MARKETING

SECTION III: STRATEGIC MARKETING

IMPERATIVE 1
Determine and Recommend Which Markets to Address

CHAPTER 7
Identifying and Choosing Opportunities

IMPERATIVE 2
Identify and Target Market Segments

CHAPTER 8
Market Segmentation and Targeting

IMPERATIVE 3
Set Strategic Direction and Positioning

CHAPTER 9
Market Strategy: Integrating Firm Efforts for Marketing Success

CHAPTER 10
Managing through the Life Cycle

CHAPTER 11
Managing Brands

SECTION IV: IMPLEMENTING THE MARKET STRATEGY

IMPERATIVE 4
Design the Market Offer

PART A: PROVIDING CUSTOMER VALUE

PART B: COMMUNICATING CUSTOMER VALUE

PART C: DELIVERING CUSTOMER VALUE

PART D: GETTING PAID FOR CUSTOMER VALUE

CHAPTER 12
Managing the Product Line

CHAPTER 15
Integrated Marketing Communications

CHAPTER 18
Distribution Decisions

CHAPTER 19
Critical Underpinnings of Pricing Decisions

CHAPTER 13
Managing Services and Customer Service

CHAPTER 16
Mass and Digital Communication

CHAPTER 20
Setting Prices

CHAPTER 14
Developing New Products

CHAPTER 17
Directing and Managing the Field Sales Effort

IMPERATIVE 5
Secure Support from Other Functions

CHAPTER 21
Ensuring the Firm Implements the Market Offer as Planned

IMPERATIVE 6
Monitor and Control

CHAPTER 22
Monitoring and Controlling Firm Functioning and Performance

SECTION V: SPECIAL MARKETING TOPICS

CHAPTER 23
International, Regional, and Global Marketing

Section III: Strategic Marketing

IMPERATIVE 1: *Determine and Recommend Which Markets to Address*

CHAPTER 7: IDENTIFYING AND CHOOSING OPPORTUNITIES

In this chapter, we address the core issue of what markets the firm/business unit should address. We begin by developing a strategy for growth.

....

A. STRATEGY FOR GROWTH

We focus on the four separate elements of a strategy for growth — vision, mission, growth path, and timing of entry.

- **VISION**. A vision is a description of an ideal future state and should be inspiring. In Figure 7A.1, state the vision for your firm/business unit. If your firm/business unit does not have a vision, or if you think the vision can be improved, state what you think the vision should be.

FIGURE 7A.1

VISION AND MISSION

Vision
Mission

- **MISSION**. Mission guides the firm/business unit's search for opportunity. Mission is normally based on a core ingredient or natural resource, technology, product or service, market or market segment, or customer needs. These bases are sometimes combined. In Figure 7A.1, state the mission for your firm/business unit. If there is no formal mission, state what you think that mission should be.
- **GROWTH PATH**. The growth path arrays various firm/business unit options in a two-dimensional matrix of market versus product/technology. In each case, the dimension is trisected — existing/related/new. Using Figure 7A.2, identify the six most recent opportunities your firm/business unit has undertaken. Based on this depiction and other information to which you have access, state the growth path for your firm/business unit — Figure 7A.3.

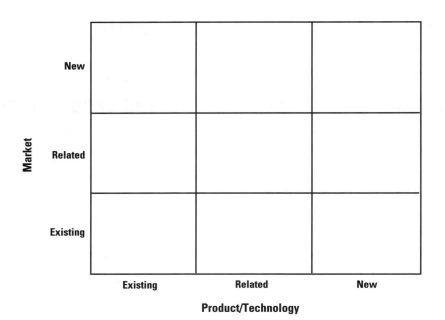

FIGURE 7A.2

GROWTH PATH MATRIX

We secure growth by…

FIGURE 7A.3

GROWTH PATH

- **TIMING OF ENTRY.** Timing of entry addresses the question of when, in the product-form life cycle, your firm/business unit tends to enter markets. There are four major options:
  - Introduction – Pioneer
  - Early growth – Follow-the-leader
  - Late growth – Segmenter
  - Maturity – Me-too

In Figure 7A.4, identify the timing-of-entry strategy that your firm/business unit prefers. What is your evidence for this strategic approach?

Timing of Entry Options	Firm/Business Unit Examples
Pioneer	
Follow-the-leader	
Segmenter	
Me-too	

FIGURE 7A.4

TIMING OF ENTRY

FIGURE 7A.5

**ASSESSING AND
RECOMMENDING
THE STRATEGY
FOR GROWTH**

Favorable Elements	Unfavorable Elements
Strategy for Growth: Recommendations	

- **ASSESSING THE STRATEGY FOR GROWTH.** In the previous exercises, you laid out the strategy for growth of your firm/business unit. In this exercise, you assess that strategy. What do you like about your firm/business unit's strategy for growth? What do you dislike about it? How do you think it should be changed? — Figure 7A.5.

B. IMPLEMENTING A STRATEGY FOR GROWTH

Essentially, your firm/business unit has seven different ways to implement a strategy for growth — internal development, insourcing, outsourcing, acquisition, strategic alliance, licensing and technology purchase, and equity investment.

- In this exercise, identify the methods your firm/business unit uses to implement the strategy for growth and state the evidence for this implementation method — Figure 7B.1.

FIGURE 7B.1

**IMPLEMENTING
A STRATEGY
FOR GROWTH**

Implementation Options	Firm/Business Unit Examples
Internal development	
Insourcing	
Outsourcing	
Acquisition	
Strategic alliance	
Licensing and technology purchase	
Equity investment	

- Assess the manner in which your firm/business unit implements its strategy for growth. What do you like about the implementation methods? What do you dislike? — Figure 7B.2.

Favorable Elements	Unfavorable Elements
Implementing a Strategy for Growth: Recommendations	

FIGURE 7B.2

ASSESSING AND RECOMMENDING GROWTH STRATEGY IMPLEMENTATION

ANALYSIS CHECK

Make sure your recommendations are supported by earlier work. In particular:

- Do they fall within the product/market scope you laid out in the preamble?
- Are they consistent with the market insight you gained in Chapter 3?
- Are they consistent with your planning assumptions in *Transition to Strategic Marketing*?

IMPERATIVE 2: *Identify and Target Market Segments*

CHAPTER 8: MARKET SEGMENTATION AND TARGETING

In Chapter 8 of your textbook, we learned about segmenting markets. Here we use a qualitative approach to developing market segments. We defined a market segment as a group of actual and potential customers with similar need profiles, seeking similar sets of benefits and values, with similar levels of priority. We must associate these similarities with identifiable customer characteristics, like age, gender, geographic location, income level, company size, and end-use application, that the firm/business unit can use as a basis for targeting communications about its offers.

Here we use six exercises designed to get you to think deeply about segmenting the market for your product, and choosing the most appropriate market segments to target for effort. Part 1 comprises five exercises:

A. Compile required customer benefits/values.

B. Brainstorm approaches to segmentation.

C. Select segmentation dimensions and form groups.

D. Develop a two-criteria segmentation grid (if required).

E. Develop the market segmentation matrix.

Part 2 focuses on selecting market segments for your firm/business unit to target.

Part 1 – Market Segmentation

A. COMPILE REQUIRED CUSTOMER BENEFITS

Return to Exercises D and E in Chapter 4 where you identified required customer benefits/values for your product in the market. See also Figure 5D.1 where you used these benefits/values to seek competitive insight. Review your work in these chapters and make any changes you think are appropriate. Note your final compilation of benefits/values in Figure 8A.1.

FIGURE 8A.1

COMPILING REQUIRED CUSTOMER BENEFITS/VALUES

1. _____   6. _____

2. _____   7. _____

3. _____   8. _____

4. _____   9. _____

5. _____   10. _____

B. BRAINSTORM APPROACHES TO SEGMENTATION

In Chapter 8 of your textbook, we showed that there were many dimensions you can use to segment a market, but only a few will likely prove useful. In this exercise, you brainstorm 10-12 segmentation dimensions that may help segment your market. Possible dimensions include:

- Age
- Gender
- Income
- Company size
- Geographic location
- End-use application
- Industry
- Annual volume potential
- Customer growth rate

Write candidate segmentation dimensions in Figure 8B.1.

FIGURE 8B.1

BRAINSTORMING APPROACHES TO SEGMENTATION

1. _____   7. _____

2. _____   8. _____

3. _____   9. _____

4. _____   10. _____

5. _____   11. _____

6. _____   12. _____

C. SELECT SEGMENTATION DIMENSIONS AND FORM GROUPS

In this exercise, you select the one or two segmentation dimensions you believe provide the greatest insight into the market and form specific groups. For example:

Age: <35 years, 35–55 years, >55 years

Gender: male, female

Industry: steel, automotive, financial services, transportation

Revenues: <$100 million; $100 million to $500 million; $501 million to $1 billion

If you believe one segmentation dimension will not suffice, select the two dimensions from Figure 8B.1 that you believe will provide you with greater insight into the market. Write down these dimensions in Figure 8C.1. Now write down the names of specific groups on these dimensions.

Dimension A._____   Segment 1. _____

Segment 2. _____

Segment 3. _____

Dimension B._____   Segment 1. _____

Segment 2. _____

Segment 3. _____

FIGURE 8C.1

SELECT SEGMENTATION DIMENSIONS AND FORM SEGMENTS

D. DEVELOP A TWO CRITERIA-GRID APPROACH TO SEGMENTATION

As suggested in Chapter 8 of your textbook, segmentation approaches often use combinations of dimensions. For example:

GENDER/AGE: male <35 years; female <35 years; male 35-55 years; female 35-55 years; male >55 years; female >55 years

INDUSTRY/REVENUES: steel/$100 million; steel/$100 million to $500 million; steel/$501 million to $1 billion: transportation; $100 million; transportation/$100 million to $500 million; transportation/$501 million to $1 billion

If you believe you require two segmentation dimensions, take the two most promising segments from Figure 8C.1 and combine them to form potential new segments:

- Using the matrix in Figure 8D.1, write in your two dimensions and segments from Figure 8C.1. (Note that the figure allows three segments for each dimension. Your dimensions may have more or fewer than three segments — just adjust the matrix accordingly.)

- Create names (or labels) for each matrix cell — segments. Write these names in the cells.

- Examine these new segments. Decide if you want to keep each of the cells as segments or whether you prefer to combine cells to form segments. If you combine cells, create a name for this new segment. Write the names of your final selection of segments in Figure 8D.2.

FIGURE 8D.1

FORMING MARKET SEGMENTS

Dimension 1:

_____

Dimension 2: _____

FIGURE 8D.2

FINAL SET OF MARKET SEGMENTS

1._____   5._____

2._____   6._____

3._____   7._____

4._____   8._____

E. DEVELOP THE MARKET SEGMENTATION MATRIX

The purpose of this exercise is to gain deeper understanding into the segments you have just formed by examining the relative importance of the various required customer benefits/values — Figure 8A.1 — in the different segments you just formed — Figure 8D.2. Remember, this exercise focuses on the benefits/values sought by customers; it has little to do with your firm/business unit's current market offerings.

- In Figure 8E.1, write the names of the segments from Figure 8D.2 across the top.

- In the left-hand column, write down the most important required customer benefits/values from Figure 8A.1.

- For each segment (column), write down the priority order of benefits/values for customers in that segment. Be prepared to add benefits/values as you focus in depth on individual segments. (To the extent that you are unsure about benefits/values and the priority orders for various segments, you are developing a marketing research agenda.)

- Examine each segment in conjunction with the others. Are the priority orders of required customer benefits/values almost identical between two segments? If so, you may want to consider collapsing these segments.

- Are you comfortable with your segmentation scheme? Can you answer _yes_ to the following questions for the segments you formed?
  - Can you _identify_ and _access_ the segments?
  - Do the segments require _differentiated_ offers?
  - Are the segments of a sufficient _size_ and potential _profitability_ to make the effort worthwhile?

Answers to these questions feed into the targeting exercise — Sections 8F–8H.

- Summarize the results in one paragraph. For example, what do you now know about the market that you didn't know before completing the analysis?

Customer Need/Required Benefits and Values	Age-Based Market Segments					

FIGURE 8E.1

MARKET SEGMENTATION MATRIX

- Among the questions that arise in this exercise are the following:

Question. How many segments should we form?

Answer. The greater the number of segments, the greater the firm/business unit's ability to deliver required benefits/values to customers in the segments. However, as the number of segments served increases, the cost of serving them also increases. The number of segments chosen is thus a compromise between delivered benefits/values, and cost. Practically speaking, it is unlikely that your firm/business unit would have the resources to develop strategies for more than a handful of segments in each market it decides to address. You should therefore limit your segmentation scheme to between five and ten segments.

Question. What is the best way to segment?

Answer. The aim of market segmentation is to develop groups of customers (segments) that have the following characteristics as regards required benefits/values: within each segment the required benefits/values are similar (homogeneous); between segments the required benefits/values are different (heterogeneous). Very often, organizations rely on history in the form of organization structure or data availability to segment markets. But the segmentation task is a creative one, and you should not feel constrained by previous decisions your firm/business unit has made.

Question. How accurate is our assessment of required customer benefits/values?

Answer. Determining required customer benefits/values is best based on marketing research. In the absence of research data, you should use managerial judgment as a first approximation, later to be substantiated by research. Customer needs are best defined in terms of benefits and values sought by customers. These benefits/values should be clearly specified. Although benefit/value terms like convenience, accuracy, and service can be valuable descriptors, they are often insufficiently precise. For example, "good service" may mean different things to different customers — speed of service, lack of hassle, or courtesy. You should push for precision.

ANALYSIS CHECK

Make sure earlier work supports your segmentation. In particular:

- Is your segmentation consistent with the customer insight you gained in Chapter 4?

- Is your segmentation based on the *right* customer type? For example, if your customer insight in Chapter 4 focused on consumers, then you should probably be segmenting consumers. However, if you decide to focus your segmentation on distribution channel customers, then go back to Chapter 4 to gain insight on those customers.

Part 2 – Targeting Market Segments

The purpose of this task is to select from the segments developed in Figure 8E.1 and identify those the firm/business unit should address. Essentially the firm/business unit chooses based on two dimensions:

- How *attractive* is the segment to the firm/business unit?

- What are the firm/business unit's *relative strengths* in the market segment, compared to competition?

The answers to these questions allow you develop a matrix to display the results.

To be in a position to select target segments, you complete three exercises:

F. Analysis of Market Segment Attractiveness

G. Business Strengths Analysis

H. Develop the Matrix Representation

F. ANALYSIS OF MARKET SEGMENT ATTRACTIVENESS

The market attractiveness exercise comprises five steps:

1. **Factor identification.** Identify general factors of market attractiveness for your firm/business unit. Examples include high market growth, few competitors, low levels of government regulation, and short payback period. Complete the following statement: "Given our history, objectives, culture, management style, successes and failures, we like to be in markets that offer … ." Brainstorm these factors using Figure 8F.1.

   When you have completed brainstorming, combine or eliminate factors until you return from five to eight factors. Enter these factors into Figure 8F.2. Describe why you included each factor. Also enter these factors in the far left column of Figure 8F.3

2. **Factor weighting.** Weight each factor in Figure 8F.3 by allocating 100 points based on its importance to the firm/business unit. Factor weights should add up to 100.

   Note that these two steps do not involve any analysis of your market segments. Your responses are general to your firm/business unit for analysis of many market opportunities. Now select the first segment for analysis. The analysis is repeated for all other segments.

3. **Market segment opportunity rating.** In Figure 8F.3, select one market segment. For each *factor*, provide a *rating* score, on a 1 to 10 scale, based on the extent to which the market segment conforms to that factor. A score of "1" implies that the market segment does not conform to the factor; a score of "10" implies high conformance. For example if the criterion is high market growth, a score of "1" may imply the segment is in decline; a score of "10" may imply that anticipated growth is very high. Scores from 2 to 9 imply intermediate growth.

4. **Develop factor scores.** In Figure 8F.3, for each factor, multiply *factor weighting* by *segment-specific rating.*

5. **Market segment attractiveness score.** In Figure 8F.3, sum the *factor scores* from step 4. This *total* number is the **market segment attractiveness** score; the range is 100 to 1,000.

6. Repeat steps 3 through 5 for the other market segments.

Note: In step 3, we suggest you perform the ratings one segment at a time, across factors. You may find it easier to complete the rating task one factor at a time, across market segments.

1.	6.
2.	7.
3.	8.
4.	9.
5.	10.
6.	12.

FIGURE 8F.1

BRAINSTORM MARKET ATTRACTIVENESS FACTORS

Market Segment Attractiveness Factor	Reasons to Include
1.	
2.	
3.	
4.	
5.	
6.	
7.	
8.	

FIGURE 8F.2

SELECTED MARKET ATTRACTIVENESS FACTORS AND REASONS TO INCLUDE

FIGURE 8F.3

ANALYSIS OF
MARKET SEGMENT
ATTRACTIVENESS

Factor	Weight	Segment: Rate	Total	Segment: Rate	Total	Segment: Rate	Total	Segment: Rate	Total
Total	100	Total		Total		Total		Total	

G: BUSINESS STRENGTHS ANALYSIS

The business strengths exercise comprises five steps. You must remember to conduct this analysis segment by segment.

1. **Factor identification.** For *each* segment, identify the business strengths (capabilities/resources) that *any competitor* would have to possess to be successful in the segment. Note that these strengths may be specific to the segment. For each segment, complete the following statement: "To be successful in this market segment, *any competitor* must possess the following business strengths (capabilities/resources)...." Brainstorm these factors using the chart in Figure 8G.1. You may examine your work in the Competitive Assessment Analysis — Figure 5D.1 — to help generate business strengths.

   When you have completed brainstorming, combine or eliminate factors until you have five to eight factors. Enter these factors into Figure 8G.2. Describe why you included each factor. Also enter these factors in the far left column of Figure 8G.3.

2. **Factor weighting.** In Figure 8G.3, weight each factor by allocating 100 points based on its importance to being successful in the market segment. Factor weights total 100.

   Note that these two steps do not involve any analysis of your firm/business unit or its competitors. Your responses are specific to the market segment, regardless of which firm/business unit is addressing the segment. Now select the first segment for analysis. You repeat the analysis for the other segment.

3. **Firm rating.** In Figure 8G.3, for each factor, *rate* your firm/business unit on its possession of these business strengths. A score of "1" implies your firm/business unit does not possess a particular strength; a score of "10" implies a high level of possession. For example, if the business strength were low-cost operations, a score of "1" implies your firm/business unit has very high costs. A score of "10" implies your firm/business unit is the low-cost producer by a considerable margin. Scores from 2 to 9 imply intermediate levels of cost competitiveness.

4. **Develop factor scores.** In Figure 8G.3, for each factor, multiply *factor weighting* by *firm/business unit rating*.

5. **Develop business strengths score.** In Figure 8G.3, sum the *factor scores* from step 4 for each factor. This *total* number is your firm/business unit's **business strengths** score for that market segment; the range is 100 to 1000.

   Repeat steps 1 through 5 for the other market segments.

Market Segment:

1. _____
2. _____
3. _____
4. _____
5. _____
6. _____
7. _____
8. _____
9. _____
10. _____

Market Segment:

1. _____
2. _____
3. _____
4. _____
5. _____
6. _____
7. _____
8. _____
9. _____
10. _____

FIGURE 8G.1

BRAINSTORM
BUSINESS
STRENGTHS
FACTORS

Market Segment:

Business Strengths Factor	Reasons to Include
1.	
2.	
3.	
4.	
5.	
6.	
7.	
8.	

Market Segment:

Business Strengths Factor	Reasons to Include
1.	
2.	
3.	
4.	
5.	
6.	
7.	
8.	

FIGURE 8G.2

SELECTED BUSINESS
STRENGTHS FACTORS
AND REASONS
TO INCLUDE

FIGURE 8G.3

BUSINESS STRENGTHS ANALYSIS

Market Segment:

Factor	Weight	Rate	Total
	100	Total	

Market Segment:

Factor	Weight	Rate	Total
	100	Total	

H. DEVELOP THE MATRIX REPRESENTATION

If you have appropriately competed part A and part B, you should have two scores for each market segment — a **market segment attractiveness** score and a **business strengths** score. Now, plot the scores for each market segment in Figure 8H.1. Answer the following questions:

1. Consider the position of each market segment you analyzed.
   - Are you surprised by any of the positions?
   - If you were surprised, what caused your surprise? Analyze scores on individual criteria to help answer this question.
   - What do these representations suggest in terms of your firm/business unit investing resources in each segment?

2. Consider what steps your firm/business unit could take to move each of the market segments to a more attractive position in the top right-hand cell of the matrix.
   - Can you improve in areas where your firm/business unit's business strengths are less than desired?
   - Is there a way to re-segment the market so that resulting segments are more attractive to your firm/business unit?

3. Summarize the results of your analysis.
   - Which market segments will your firm/business unit target? Why?
   - Which market segments will your firm/business unit not target? Why?

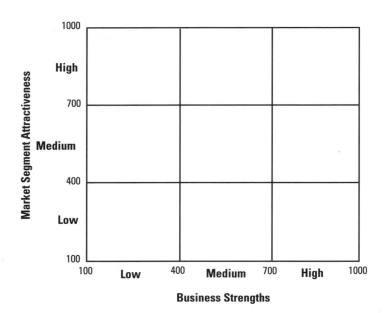

FIGURE 8H.1

MARKET SEGMENT ATTRACTIVENESS/ BUSINESS STRENGTHS MATRIX

IMPERATIVE 3: *Set Strategic Direction and Positioning*

CHAPTER 9: MARKET STRATEGY: INTEGRATING FIRM EFFORTS FOR MARKETING SUCCESS

In Chapter 8, you segmented the market for your product and decided which segments to target for firm/business unit effort. In this chapter, you lay out a market strategy for each segment that you targeted. For background information, refer to Chapter 9 in your textbook. If you decided to target multiple market segments, you should conduct the following process for each segment. The market segment strategy comprises four separate elements:

A. Objectives

B. Strategic Focus

C. Positioning

D. Implications for Implementing Action Programs

A: OBJECTIVES

Objective setting comprises two separate decisions — choice of *strategic objectives* and choice of *operational objectives.*

STRATEGIC OBJECTIVES. You must select your strategic objectives from among a relatively limited set. You should anticipate that these objectives will be in place for the next three years:

- Consider such dimensions as revenue growth, market share growth, improving profits, and generating cash flow.
- State which of your objectives is the most important — primary objective, and which is the second-most important — secondary objective.

OPERATIONAL OBJECTIVES. You must set target performance levels for your strategic objectives. Be clear how you will measure your performance — in absolute numbers, as a growth rate, or as a yield percent (e.g., ROI).

Now you combine strategic and operational objectives into an overall statement of objectives.

An example is: "During the next three years we will increase profits from nucleopolyamide sales to independent molders from $15 million in 20XY to $25 million in 20XY+3."

Use Figure 9A.1 for laying out the objectives for each segment you decided to target.

FIGURE 9A.1

OBJECTIVES
FOR THE MARKET
STRATEGY

		Segment:	Segment:	Segment:
Strategic Objectives	Primary			
	Secondary			
Operational Objectives	Primary			
	Secondary			
Overall Statement of Objectives				

B: STRATEGIC FOCUS

The strategic focus states generally how you intend to achieve your objectives. The strategic focus comprises two separate elements — *unit sales volume* and *improving margins and investment returns*. In each case, there are four broad options:

Increase Unit Sales Volume	Improve Margins and Investment Returns
Current Customers Increase customer retention Increase customer use	**Increase Revenues** Raise prices Improve the sales mix
New Customers Attract customers from competitors Secure new business	**Costs and Assets** Reduce operating costs Improve asset utilization

Use Figure 9B.1 to state your strategic focus for each target market segment. For each segment, describe briefly the broad focus of your efforts — in other words, how you intend to achieve your objectives.

Continuing the previous example: "We will achieve our objectives by targeting those molders that have had little experience with nucleopolyamide. Specifically, we will show them that nucleopolyamide molding offers substantial opportunities for growth and profit."

Note the statement of strategic focus has two parts:

1. A brief description of what, generally, you intend to do
2. A clear description of how you intend to do it

	Segment:	Segment:	Segment:
What you intend to do			
How you intend to do it			

FIGURE 9B.1

STRATEGIC FOCUS

C: POSITIONING

For each target market segment, you must make a positioning decision. Positioning requires that you make decisions on three key dimensions — customer targets, competitive targets, and value proposition. You must also state why your customer targets should believe that you will deliver on your value proposition — reason to believe. Use Figure 9C.1 to identify the positioning elements for each target market segment.

CUSTOMER TARGETS. Customer targets are the organizations and individuals you intend to influence so they behave in such a way that your firm/business unit attains its objectives. You must consider both purchase decision-makers and influentials — Chapter 4. The specific behaviors you require may be purchase or recommendation to purchase.

Continuing our previous example: "Our major efforts will be focused in providing technical assistance both to manufacturing personnel at the molders and to product engineers at the appliance/automobile manufacturers."

COMPETITOR TARGETS. Competitor targets are the organizations and individuals that have customer targets similar to your firm/business unit — Chapter 5. Recall that you can frame competitors in several different ways:

- Comparison with individual direct competitor — "7-Up tastes better than Sprite."
- Product form superiority — "7-Up, the best-tasting lemon-lime soda,"
- Out of product form — "7-Up, the uncola,"
- Implied or claimed uniqueness — "7-Up, the real thing, the only one," etc.

Continuing the example: "Our major efforts will be directed against key domestic competitors that produce alternative forms of nucleopolyamide, specifically Dow and DuPont. Secondarily, we will build a defensive position against Hoechst and Bayer — we anticipate these firms will enter the market with new technology during the next three years."

VALUE PROPOSITION. The value proposition represents key customer benefits/values your firm/business unit will deliver that will cause your customer targets to behave in the way you require, rather than be influenced by a competitor. The value proposition should exploit the differential advantage you have over competitor targets. The value proposition should communicate, in a clear and concise way, the key benefits/values your customer targets will realize.

To continue with the example: "Our value proposition for the molders is to demonstrate to their plant managers that use of Zytene increases throughput. Specifically, we shall show that by using Zytene, rather than Nuclan (DuPont), molding time is reduced, cleaning time is reduced because of fewer deposits in the mold, and the need to clean flashing from the part is eliminated. For appliance and automobile product engineers, we shall demonstrate that parts made with Zytene fail less frequently than those made with Nuclan."

REASON TO BELIEVE. In the value proposition, you state the key customer benefits/values your firm/business unit will deliver. But why should customers believe you can deliver on these benefits/values? The *reason-to-believe* statement answers this question.

To continue with the example: "We have completed extensive field tests with a wide variety of molders, under a wide variety of conditions — the national molders association has certified these tests. For appliance and automobile engineers, we have conducted extensive laboratory tests and have made public the results."

FIGURE 9C.1

POSITIONING ELEMENTS

	Segment:	Segment:	Segment:
Customer Targets			
Competitor Targets			
Value Proposition			
Reason to Believe			

POSITIONING STATEMENT. For each segment, take the positioning elements and formulate a comprehensive positioning statement using the chart in Figure 9C.2. We will:

Convince	[customer target]
In the context of other alternatives	[competitor target]
That they will receive these benefits	[value proposition]
Because we have these capabilities/resources	[reason to believe]

FIGURE 9C.2

POSITIONING STATEMENTS

Segment:

We will convince...	
...**that**... (in the context of other alternatives)	
...**that**... (they will receive these benefits)	
...**because**... (we have these capabilities/resources)	

Segment:

We will convince...	
...**that**... (in the context of other alternatives)	
...**that**... (they will receive these benefits)	
...**because**... (we have these capabilities/resources)	

ANALYSIS CHECK

To make sure that earlier work supports each market segment strategy, conduct the following tests:

- Are the objectives consistent with your market insight — Chapter 3?
- Is the strategic focus consistent with what you learned about the value of customers — Chapter 2?
- Is the positioning consistent with your customer insight — Chapter 4?
- Is the positioning consistent with your competitor insight — Chapter 5? In particular, does the value proposition address important customer needs?

D: IMPLICATIONS FOR IMPLEMENTING ACTION PROGRAMS

IMPLICATIONS. For each target segment, the positioning statement has implications for several marketing implementation actions. Using Figure 9E.1, identify broad implications of your positioning statement for action programs:

- **Product.** Which products should receive primary attention? Which products should be de-emphasized? What degree of product acceptance exists at present? How do your products compare with those offered by competitors?
- **Service.** What level of service do customers desire; what are they willing to pay for? How does this service level differ from your current service?
- **Promotion.** What elements of the promotional mix will you require to implement the proposed positioning? What particular requirements will you place on your selling effort? How will you orchestrate all your promotional options to communicate effectively with customers and enhance the strength of your offer?
- **Distribution.** What unique role will distribution play in helping you achieve your objectives? What are customer expectations; what must you do to meet these expectations? What special delivery, stocking, or other considerations should you consider for implementing the proposed positioning?
- **Pricing.** What role will price play in your proposed positioning? How can you augment the value of your offer to enhance the potential for obtaining better pricing? How will you use pricing competitively? How may pricing in this segment affect pricing in other segments?
- **Functional support.** What kinds of support will you require from non-marketing functions? How can you ensure such support? What are the behavioral, political, and technical issues you must resolve to secure this support?

Answers to these and comparable questions will help you frame the programs you will need to implement and execute your market strategy.

Segment:	Segment:
Product	Product
Service	Service
Promotion	Promotion
Distribution	Distribution
Price	Price
Functional support	Functional support

FIGURE 9E.1

IMPLICATIONS FOR IMPLEMENTING ACTION PROGRAMS

CHAPTER 10: MANAGING THROUGH THE LIFE CYCLE

In Chapter 3, you examined the life cycle for the product form to which your product belongs. In this chapter you use your work from Chapter 3 to clarify the life-cycle stage and also assess your competitive position. You make a choice of strategic option your firm/business unit should pursue.

A. LIFE-CYCLE STRATEGY

PRODUCT LIFE-CYCLE STAGE. Clarify the current stage of the product-form life cycle. You should select from the following options:
- Introduction
- Early Growth
- Late Growth
- Maturity
- Decline

LIFE-CYCLE SCENARIOS. Combine the life-cycle stage you just selected with your competitive position. Of the nine scenarios listed below, select the one that best captures the situation your product now faces:
- Scenario 1: Introduction Stage: The Pioneers
- Scenario 2: Early Growth Leaders
- Scenario 3: Early Growth Followers
- Scenario 4: Late Growth Stage
- Scenario 5: Growth in a Mature Market
- Scenario 6: Leaders in Concentrated Mature Markets
- Scenario 7: Followers in Concentrated Mature Markets
- Scenario 8: Mature Fragmented Markets
- Scenario 9: Markets in Decline

STRATEGIC OPTIONS. Each life-cycle scenario offers several different strategic options:
- Scenario 1:
    - Build low-cost barriers via penetration pricing
    - Exploit first-mover advantages
- Scenario 2:
    - Continue to be leader — enhance position
    - Continue to be leader — maintain position
    - Surrender leadership — retreat to a market segment or segments
    - Surrender leadership — exit the market
- Scenario 3:
    - Seek market leadership
    - Settle for second place
    - Focus on a market segment or segments
    - Exit the market
- Scenario 4
    - Address many market segments
    - Address few market segments
- Scenario 5
    - Find creative ways to drive growth
- Scenario 6
    - Maintain leadership over the long run
    - Harvest
- Scenario 7
    - Improve market position
    - Keep on truckin'
    - Exit

- Scenario 8
  - Acquisition
  - Standardization and branding
- Scenario 9
  - Leadership
  - Harvest, divest, segment
  - Leverage the brand

We discuss the rationales for analyzing strategic options in Chapter 10 of your textbook. Complete Figure 10A.1, identifying your position in terms of product life-cycle stage and scenario. Select a strategic option and provide the rationale.

Product Life-Cycle Stage	Scenario	Selected Strategic Option
Rationale		

FIGURE 10A.1

STRATEGIC OPTIONS
IN THE PRODUCT
LIFE CYCLE

ANALYSIS CHECK

To make sure that earlier work supports your life-cycle strategy, conduct the following tests:

- Does your product life-cycle analysis support the life-cycle strategy — Chapter 3?
- Are your planning assumptions consistent with the life-cycle strategy — Chapter 6?
- Is your strategy for growth consistent with the life cycle-strategy — Chapter 7?

CHAPTER 11: MANAGING BRANDS

In this chapter, we focus on branding. You may choose as your focus the product brand, a masterbrand (family brand), or the corporate brand.

A: BRAND IDENTITY

First, we clarify your brand identity. Brand identity is the outward expression of the brand — *what you want* the brand to mean to customers. Using Figure 11A.1, state your brand identity in a single sentence.

FIGURE 11A.1

BRAND IDENTITY

B: BRAND ASSOCIATIONS AND BRAND IMAGE

If you have done a good job of branding, the associations *customers have* of your brand should relate strongly to brand identity. Customers' brand image then mirrors brand identity. In this exercise, you survey a few customers in your target segment to assess the associations they have about your brand. Specifically:

- Interview a few customers and have them free-associate with your brand. Place these associations in Figure 11B.1.

- Based on these associations, write a one-sentence statement of the image customers hold about your brand — Figure 11B.2.

FIGURE 11B.1

BRAND ASSOCIATIONS

1._____ 11._____

2._____ 12._____

3._____ 13._____

4._____ 14._____

5._____ 15._____

6._____ 16._____

7._____ 17._____

8._____ 18._____

9._____ 19._____

10._____ 20._____

FIGURE 11B.2

BRAND IMAGE

C: THE BRAND IDENTITY AND BRAND IMAGE GAP

At this point, we step back and explore the gap between **brand identity** and **brand image**. If brand identity and brand image are different, you have to do some work to make brand image conform to brand identity.

- Examine the gap between **brand identity** — Figure 11A.1 — and **brand image** — Figure 11B.2. Specify the key areas you should change — Figure 11C.1.

- Also in Figure 11C.1, lay out a tentative program for bringing **brand identity** and **brand image** into alignment.

Branding elements you should change

FIGURE 11C.1

GAP BETWEEN
BRAND IDENTITY
AND BRAND IMAGE

Tentative approach for aligning brand identity and brand image

D: BRAND POSITIONING STATEMENT

The final element in the branding exercises is to develop a **brand positioning statement** for your brand. As input, you have already developed some tentative ideas on how to bring **brand image** into alignment with **brand identity**. The final step is to join those ideas with the reality of the market, considering competitors and other market factors. Write this statement in Figure 11D.1.

FIGURE 11D.1

BRAND
POSITIONING
STATEMENT

ANALYSIS CHECK

Make sure earlier work supports your branding strategy by conducting the following tests:

- Is the branding strategy consistent with your market, customer, competitor, firm, and complementer insight — Chapters 3, 4, 5, and 6?
- Is the branding strategy consistent with your market strategy — Chapter 9?

Managing Marketing in the 21ˢᵗ Century

Section IV: Implementing the Market Strategy

IMPERATIVE 4: *Design the Market Offer*

Part A: Providing Customer Value

CHAPTER 12: MANAGING THE PRODUCT LINE

Although not always the case, the firm/business unit's product is often the major basis for providing customer value and securing differential advantage. In this chapter, we explore several product-related issues by examining the relationships of your product with other products in the product line.

....

A. INTERRELATIONSHIPS ABOUT RESOURCES

Within any organization, there is always a tussle for various types of resources. A useful approach for addressing resource allocation issues is the **product portfolio matrix**. In this matrix (aka growth-share matrix) you array different products in your firm/business unit's product line. Key dimensions are long-run market growth rate and relative market share. You can then assess resource allocation for your product:

- In Figure 12A.1, identify the various products (or product groups) in your firm/business unit.
- For each entry, assess long-run (three-to-five-year) market growth rate.
- Note your firm/business unit's sales revenues and market share.
- Note your strongest competitor's sales revenues and market share.
- Calculate your firm/business unit's relative market share.

Firm/ Business Unit Product	Market Growth Rate	Sales Revenues	Market Share	Strongest Competitor's Product	Sales Revenue	Market Share	Firm/ Business Unit Product RMS

FIGURE 12A.1

RELATIVE MARKET SHARE (RMS) CALCULATIONS

- Plot your firm/business unit's products in the long-run growth rate/relative market share matrix — Figure 12A.2. To construct this matrix, you should develop the scale that makes sense to you in the environment your firm/business unit operates. In general the mid-point on the long-run market growth axis should be a little above GDP growth.

FIGURE 12A.2

GROWTH/SHARE MATRIX

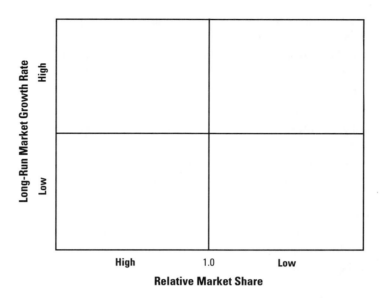

FIGURE 12A.2

GROWTH/SHARE MATRIX

- Based on the matrix you developed in Figure 12A.2, what is your assessment of the level and type of resources the firm/business unit is allocating to your product compared to other products in the portfolio? Are they reasonable, or should they be increased? What arguments can you make for changes — Figure 12A.3?

FIGURE 12A.3

ASSESSMENT OF RESOURCE ALLOCATION FOR YOUR PRODUCT

Type of Resouces	Level of Allocation	Arguments for Change (if any)

B. IMPROVING THE PRODUCT OFFERING

In this section, we focus on improving the product offering. We ask you to think of tactics you could employ that would not only provide greater customer value, but would also increase revenues and profits. Here are some questions to get you started:

- Are there options to introduce products that complement the products you now offer?
- Are there products your firm/business unit now offers that negatively affect sales of your product, because of the way customers view them? If so, what should you do?

- Are there opportunities to add additional products to fill out your product line? What is the nature of these opportunities?

- Are some of the products that your firm/business unit offers earning less than a desirable financial return? Should you drop some products from your product line?

- How do you assess the quality of your products? Where are improvements possible?

- Are there any product-safety issues your firm/business unit should address?

- Do you sell your product as a stand-alone item, or is it bundled with other products? Are there opportunities for bundling/unbundling?

- Are used products sold in a secondary market? What is the impact of this secondary marketing on sales of your products in the primary market? What actions could you take?

- Does your firm/business unit face any counterfeiting problems? How can you address these problems?

- To what extent can packaging be a way to add customer value? What options do you have to add value by packaging?

- Are you facing any problems of product disposal when your product is used? What are the options for dealing with these problems? Are there re-use/recycling possibilities for the product? Can you use these to add value?

ANALYSIS CHECK

Make sure that previous decisions support your approach to improving the product offering. Ask whether your approaches for product improvement support the market strategy — Chapter 9.

CHAPTER 13: MANAGING SERVICES AND CUSTOMER SERVICE

Whether the focus of your project is a physical product or a service, there are, no doubt, many service elements associated with your market offer. In this chapter, we address these service elements.

A. DELIVERING SERVICES

To deliver services to customers, you require service facilities. In your textbook, we identified these as *on-stage* and *off-stage*, service equipment, service personnel, and optional service guarantees.

- Using Figure 13A.1, identify the various elements in each service category, assess their quality, and make suggestions for improvement.

FIGURE 13A.1

SERVICE DELIVERY RESOURCES

Service Resource	Description	Quality of Service Resource	Suggestions for Improvement
Facilities: *on-stage*			
Facilities: *off-stage*			
Equipment			
People			
Guarantees			

B. THE SERVICE BLUEPRINT

In Figure 13.1 in your textbook, we laid out an example of a service blueprint. In this exercise, you use the blueprint concept to chart out a service that you deliver to customers. You then seek to identify ways of improving your service delivery system.

In Figure 13B.1, chart out the elements of your service delivery system. In Figure 13B.2, identify the critical elements of this system from a customer perspective, assess your firm/business unit's current performance, and suggest ways for improvement.

FIGURE 13B.1

CHARTING THE SERVICE BLUEPRINT

Service Delivery Item	Description	Assessment	Improvement Options

FIGURE 13B.2

ASSESSING THE SERVICE BLUEPRINT

C. SERVICE QUALITY

In this exercise, we examine your firm/business unit's service quality. We assess both customer expectations of service quality and their perceptions of the firm/business unit's service quality.

Use the 22-Item SERVQUAL scale in Figure 13C.1 to collect data from customers on their expectations and perceptions of service quality. You may want to place your survey instrument on *www.surveymonkey.com* as a data collection device.

ServQual Dimensions	Servqual Expectations Item	Servqual Perception Item	Score
TANGIBLES	1. Excellent _____ companies will have modern-looking equipment.	XYZ has modern-looking equipment.	
	2. The physical facilities at excellent _____ companies will be visually appealing.	XYZ's physical facilities are visually appealing.	
	3. Employees at excellent _____ companies will be neat-appearing.	XYZ are neat-appearing.	
	4. Material associated with the service (such as pamphlets or statements) will be visually appealing in an excellent _____ company.	Material associated with the service (such as pamphlets or statements) is visually appealing at XYZ.	
REALIABILITY	5. When excellent _____ companies promise to do something by a certain time, they will do so.	When XYZ promises to do something by a certain time, it does so.	
	6. When a customer has a problem, excellent _____ companies will show a sincere interest in solving it.	When you have a problem, XYZ shows a sincere interest in solving it.	
	7. Excellent _____ companies will perform the service right the first time.	XYZ performs the service right the first time.	
	8. Excellent _____ companies will provide their services at the time they promise to do so.	XYZ provides its services at the time it promises to do so.	
	9. Excellent _____ companies will insist on error-free records.	XYZ insists on error-free records.	
RESPONSIVENESS	10. Employees in excellent _____ companies will tell customers exactly when services will be performed.	Employees in XYZ tell you exactly when services will be performed.	
	11. Employees in excellent _____ companies will give prompt service to customers.	Employees in XYZ give you prompt service.	
	12. Employees in excellent _____ companies will always be willing to help customers.	Employees in XYZ are always willing to help you.	
	13. Employees in excellent _____ companies will never be too busy to respond to customers' requests.	Employees in XYZ are never too busy to respond to your requests.	

FIGURE 13C.1

THE 22-ITEM SERVQUAL SCALE

CONTINUES ON NEXT PAGE

FIGURE 13C.1

(CONTINUED)

ServQual Dimensions	Servqual Expectations Item	Servqual Perception Item	Score
ASSURANCE	14. The behavior of employees in excellent _____ companies will instill confidence in customers.	The behavior of employees in XYZ instills confidence in you.	
	15. Customers of excellent _____ companies will feel safe in their transactions.	You feel safe in your transactions with XYZ.	
	16. Employees in excellent _____ companies will be consistently courteous with customers.	Employees in XYZ are consistently courteous with you.	
	17. Employees in excellent _____ companies will have the knowledge to answer customers' questions.	Employees in XYZ have the knowledge to answer your questions.	
EMPATHY	18. Excellent _____ companies will give customers individual attention.	XYZ gives you individual attention.	
	19. Excellent _____ companies will have operating hours convenient to all their customers.	XYZ has operating hours convenient to all its customers.	
	20. Excellent _____ companies will have employees who give customers personal attention.	XYZ has employees who give you personal attention.	
	21. Excellent _____ companies will have the customer's best interests at heart.	XYZ has your best interests at heart.	
	22. The employees of excellent _____ companies will understand the specific needs of their customers.	Employees of XYZ understand your specific needs.	

All questions should be answered on a 1 to 7 scale: 1 = Strongly Disagree, 7 = Strongly Agree.

- From the survey results, calculate the *expectations* and *perception* scores for each of the five service quality dimensions by summing the constituent scores:
  - Tangibles
  - Reliability
  - Responsiveness
  - Assurance
  - Empathy
- Plot the results in Figure 13C.2. Make your own decision on numbering the axes.

FIGURE 13C.2

THE SERVICE QUALITY CHART

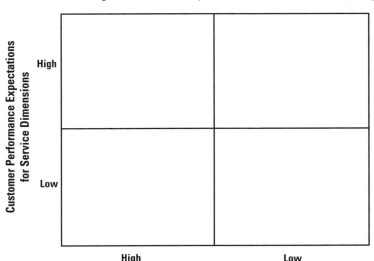

D. IMPROVING SERVICE DELIVERY

Based on your analysis in Section 13A — Delivering Services, Section 13B — The Service Blueprint, and Section 13C — Service Quality, place your recommendations for improving service in Figure 13D.1.

Recommendations

ANALYSIS CHECK

Make sure that prior analysis and other decisions you have made are consistent with, and supportive of, your recommendations for improving service delivery:

- Are your service improvement recommendations consistent with your customer insight — Chapter 4?
- Are your service improvement recommendations supportive of the market strategy — Chapter 9?
- Are your service improvement recommendations consistent with other marketing implementation actions — Chapters 12, 14, 15, 16, 17, 18, 19, and 20?

CHAPTER 14: DEVELOPING NEW PRODUCTS

In this chapter, we shift focus to the issue of developing new products. We focus on the new product development process. You also generate ideas for new products.

A. NEW PRODUCT DEVELOPMENT PROCESS

Your textbook identifies several stages in the new product development process: idea generation, preliminary screening, concept development, business-case analysis, development, product testing, market-factor testing, test marketing, and commercialization. In this section, you briefly describe and assess each stage, and then offer ideas for improvement — Figure 14A.1.

FIGURE 14A.1

NEW PRODUCT
DEVELOPMENT
PROCESS

Stage	Description of Firm/Business Unit Approach	Assessment of Firm/Business Unit Approach	Ideas for Improvement
Idea generation			
Preliminary screening			
Concept development			
Business-case analysis			
Development			
Product testing			
Market-factor testing			
Test marketing			
Commercialization			

B. IDEA GENERATION

Your textbook identifies several approaches for generating new product ideas. Select one or more of these approaches, be creative, and identify some new product ideas. Use Figure 14B.1 to generate new ideas. Which of these ideas has the most promise? Why? What resources may be required to exploit the new idea?

FIGURE 14B.1

NEW PRODUCT IDEAS
USING MULTIPLE
APPROACHES

Approach to Identifying New Product Ideas	New Product Ideas	Best Idea	Why Best Idea?	Resource Implications?
Structured Thinking				
Attribute listing				
Morphological analysis				
Unstructured Thinking				
Brainstorming				
Mind mapping				
Provocation				
Random input				
Six Thinking Hats				

C. IDEA GENERATION USING THE IDEA GENERATOR

One of the more promising methods for new idea generation is the idea generator. Starting with your current product, apply one or more of the five operations to identify new ideas:

Innovation Template	Definition
Subtraction	Remove components, particularly the desirable or even indispensable
Multiplication	Make one or more copies of an existing component
Division	Divide an existing product into its component parts
Task unification	Assign a new task to an existing element
Attribute dependency change	Involves dependent relationships between product attributes and attributes of its immediate environment

Use Figure 14C.1 to develop new ideas. Which of these ideas has the most promise? Why? What resources would your firm/business unit require to exploit the idea?

Innovation Template	New Product Ideas	Best Idea	Why Best Idea?	Resource Implications?
Subtraction				
Multiplication				
Division				
Task unification				
Attribute dependency change				

FIGURE 14C.1

THE IDEA GENERATOR

ANALYSIS CHECK

A formal part of the process is to be sure that your approach to developing new products supports previous decisions. Ask yourself these questions:

- Does your firm/business unit approach support the market strategy — Chapter 9?
- Is your approach consistent with the approach to improving the product offering — Chapter 12?

Part B: Communicating Customer Value

CHAPTER 15: INTEGRATED MARKETING COMMUNICATIONS

In Chapter 9, you developed a product/market strategy; in Chapter 11, you developed an accompanying brand positioning statement. In this chapter, you focus on developing a communications strategy for your product and brand, as well as an implementation plan.

A. THE COMMUNICATIONS STRATEGY

As we discussed in Chapter 15 of your textbook, the communications strategy requires the firm/business unit to answer six basic questions:

1. Who are our communications targets?
2. What are our communications objectives?
3. What key message do we want to get across?
4. What communications tools shall we use?
5. What communications budget shall we set?
6. When is the *right* time to communicate?

Each of these questions gives rise to many subsidiary questions.

COMMUNICATIONS TARGETS. You must decide the particular customer target(s) you want to address with your communications. If your firm/business unit is a B2C marketer, your communications target may be consumers, but it may also be organizations in the distribution channel. If you are a B2B marketer, the audience could be a customer or even your own sales force. Of course, you may decide to address multiple audiences with the same communications strategy; for example, consumers, distribution channel members, and shareholders. When you have multiple audiences, some will probably be primary targets and others secondary targets. Your communications targets should flow from the market strategy that you developed in Chapter 9. Identify your communications targets in the top line of Figure 15A.1.

FIGURE 15A.1

THE COMMUNICATIONS STRATEGY

	Target 1:	Target 2:	Target 3:
Objectives			
Key messages			
Tools			
Budget ($)			
Timing			

COMMUNICATIONS OBJECTIVES. For each communications target, you should be very clear about what you want the communications to achieve. There are many possible objectives; these range between obtaining customer awareness and achieving customer retention. Consult Chapter 15 in your textbook for a discussion of communications objectives. Write in communications objectives for your various market targets in Figure 15A.1.

COMMUNICATIONS MESSAGES. Constructing the message is central to the communications strategy. Messages should reflect the value proposition in the market strategy. Likely, different communication targets require different messages.

COMMUNICATIONS TOOLS. In Chapter 17, we focus on communications from the sales force. In this chapter, we focus on other communications tools. Mostly these will be mass communications, digital, or word-of-mouth. Write in the communications tools you plan on using to reach your various market targets — Figure 15A.1.

COMMUNICATIONS BUDGET. You must decide the size of your communications budget. Clearly, the budget will be related to your overall market strategy — Chapter 9 — and your communications objectives. Write your communications budget for each communications target in Figure 15A.1.

TIMING. You must decide the right time to implement your communications strategy.

ANALYSIS CHECK

Make sure that previous decisions support your communications strategy, in particular the market strategy — Chapter 9, and branding decisions — Chapter 11.

- Are the communications targets consistent with your choices of:
  - Target market segments — Chapter 8?
  - Customer choices in the strategic focus — Chapter 9?
  - Customer targets in the positioning statement — Chapter 9?
  - Competitor targets in the positioning statement — Chapter 9?
- Are your communications objectives consistent with your strategic and operational objectives — Chapter 9?
- Is your messaging consistent with *positioning* in the market strategy?
- Are the communications tools you selected able to communicate the value proposition effectively — Chapter 9?
- Is your communications budget consistent with the market strategy — Chapter 9?
- Are your communications consistent with the brand positioning — Chapter 11?
- Is your communications timing consistent with predictable but uncontrollable events, and with other marketing implementation actions? Refer to Chapters 12, 13, 14, 16, 17, 18, 19, and 20.

CHAPTER 16: MASS AND DIGITAL COMMUNICATION

As discussed in Chapter 16 of your textbook, the **creative brief** is the vehicle by which a product or marketing manager communicates his/her vision of the firm/business unit's communications to a target audience. The manager transmits the vision, outlined in the creative brief, to those charged with coming up with ideas and actually developing the communications. In many cases, the *creatives* are advertising agency employees.

Recall that the firm should develop a creative brief for any communication it plans to use. These communications encompass all conventional print and visual media, but also includes direct mail, Internet communications, and publicity and public relations.

In Chapter 15, you identified several customer targets you wanted to address with communications. You also identified your communications objectives, messages, tools, budget, and timing for each communications target.

Your textbook also noted that the firm frequently develops two creative briefs: one for the campaign idea, the second for executions of a campaign idea on which the firm/business unit and the advertising agency have agreed. In this exercise, you develop the creative brief for a campaign idea.

A. DEVELOPING CAMPAIGN IDEAS

DEVELOP THE CREATIVE BRIEF. The creative brief comprises eight elements identified in your textbook — Chapter 16. Draw on your previous analysis, especially from Chapters 9 and 11, to develop a creative brief for each target audience. Remember the elements are as follows:

- **Marketing objective.** What the firm/business unit wants to achieve — output and intermediate objectives.
- **Assignment.** The type of campaign including media type, timing, and approval process.
- **Customer insight.** Informs the creative process — critical insight into target market; identifies rational and emotional factors that drive product purchase/use.
- **Competitive insight.** Informs the creative process — includes barriers to achieving firm/business unit objectives.
- **Target audience.** Whom the firm/business unit wishes to influence — customer types and segments, includes demographics, psychographics, and current products.
- **Key benefit.** The most important benefit/value the firm/business unit wishes to emphasize.
- **Reasons to believe.** Why the target customer should believe firm/business unit claims.
- **Brand identity.** How the firm/business unit wants the target audience to feel about its product. Should be important to the audience, deliverable by the firm/business unit, and unique to the brand.
- **Mandates.** Elements outside the advertiser's control — must or must not be included, like corporate and/or legal requirements advertising must meet.
- **Measurement.** How the firm/business unit will know if the campaign has been successful.

Lay out your creative brief in Figure 16A.1.

FIGURE 16A.1

DEVELOP THE CREATIVE BRIEF

Target Audience: _____

Marketing Objective	
Assignment	
Customer Insight	
Competitive Insight	
Key Benefit	
Reasons to Believe	
Brand Identity	
Mandates	
Measurement	

ASSESS THE CREATIVE BRIEF PROCESS. Developing a creative brief is not a simple task. Identify the top three issues you had to address while developing your creative brief for a campaign idea — Figure 16A.2

1.
2.
3.

FIGURE 16A.2

TOP THREE ISSUES
IN DEVELOPING THE
CREATIVE BRIEF FOR
A CAMPAIGN IDEA

DEVELOP A CAMPAIGN IDEA. Based on the creative brief you just produced, develop two different campaign ideas that satisfy the criteria you laid out in the creative brief. Record your campaign ideas — Figure 16A.3.

Campaign Idea 1:	Campaign Idea 2:

FIGURE 16A.3

TWO CAMPAIGN IDEAS

ASSESS THE CAMPAIGN IDEAS. How good are your campaign ideas? In this exercise, you use Figure 16A.4 to assess the quality of your campaign ideas on several dimensions.

	Campaign Idea 1:	Campaign Idea 2:
Accomplishes the objective		
Communicates the product and brand positioning		
Is believable, unique, competitive, ownable		
Is effective for the intended communications target		
Is provocative – the target will pay attention		
Has "legs" – is campaignable		
Doesn't alienate any other communication targets		

FIGURE 16A.4

ASSESSING
CAMPAIGN IDEAS

B. MEDIA SCHEDULE

In the interest of optimizing your learning, we halted the previous exercise at developing a campaign idea and did not push through to actual advertisement; that level of detail is more appropriate for an advertising or integrated communications course. For this exercise, we assume you are managing the market strategy, using advertising as one of many communications options, and that the agency has developed the advertisements you wanted. If you do not plan to use advertising, please skip to the analysis check.

In the communications strategy — Figure 15A.1 — you identified communications tools — media classes you would use. In addition, you specified the media budget for each communications target. Now is the time to allocate your media budget across the various media classes — TV, print, direct marketing, publicity & public relations, and sales promotion — and to select specific media vehicles in those classes. Make sure to include digital media options like online advertising and public relations, blogs and microblogs, social media, and mobile marketing.

BUDGET ALLOCATION BY MEDIA CLASS. Return to your communications budget for a specific communications target — Figure 15A.1. In Figure 16B.1, identify how you will allocate this budget across the various media classes.

BUDGET ALLOCATION BY MEDIA VEHICLE. Also in Figure 16B.1, identify the various media vehicles you will use in each media class, and specify how you will allocate the media class budgets to the various media vehicles within that class. Use the Internet to identify media costs to help make your allocations.

FIGURE 16B.1

ALLOCATING THE
COMMUNICATIONS
BUDGET

Communications Target: _____   Communications Budget: $_____

Media Class	Media Class Budget	Media Vehicle	Media Vehicle Budget

SCHEDULING THE COMMUNICATIONS. The final task is to schedule the media. There are many influences on the schedule, not the least of which is media availability and seasonal effects. For this exercise, we do not ask you to schedule by the week or day, but rather to make a first cut at scheduling by the month. Use Figure 16B.2 to schedule your media vehicles by month.

Media Class: _____   Budget for Media Class: $_____

Media Vehicle	Jan.	Feb.	March	April	May	June	July	Aug.	Sept.	Oct.	Nov.	Dec.	Vehicle Budget

Media Class Budget: $_____

C. EVALUATING THE COMMUNICATIONS PROGRAM

In the previous exercises, you laid out a communications strategy and a partial implementation plan, using a creative brief for a campaign idea and, perhaps, a media-planning schedule.

Chapter 16 in your textbook discusses several different measures of advertising effectiveness. In Figure 16C.1, describe what measures you will use to test the success of your campaigns, and how you intend to go about evaluating your communications program.

Evaluation Measures	Evaluation Method

ANALYSIS CHECK

In this exercise, test that your mass and digital communications are consistent with the communications strategy you created previously — Chapter 15:

- Is the creative brief consistent with your communications strategy? In particular, does the brief clearly communicate your requirements in terms of communications targets and communications objectives?
- Is the media schedule consistent with your communications budget and timing requirements?
- Will your evaluation measures appropriately capture the success of your mass and digital communications?

CHAPTER 17: DIRECTING AND MANAGING THE FIELD SALES EFFORT

In this chapter, we address several questions relating to the six tasks of sales management discussed in your textbook. Please refer to Chapter 17 for background. To start, you should sketch out the current sales force system for your product.

A. CURRENT SALES FORCE SYSTEM

As a starting point for directing and managing the field sales effort, sketch out the current sales force system — Figure 17A.1. Among the items you should address are:

- Number of salespeople
- Reporting relationships from salespeople to district managers, district managers to regional sales managers, regional sales managers to national sales manager, and so forth. Include numbers of managers in each position.
- Presence/absence of program for strategic/key accounts.
- Sales force organization — for example, by geography, product, market segment
- Salespeople competence — consider recruiting, selecting, training, coaching, turnover rates
- Sales manager competence — consider recruiting, selecting, training, coaching, turnover rates
- Recent performance — sales growth, market share gains/losses, new product introductions, etc.

FIGURE 17A.1

SKETCH OF SALES FORCE SYSTEM

B. SALES OBJECTIVES

In earlier chapters, you laid out marketing objectives for your product. In this exercise, you translate marketing objectives into quantitative objectives for the sales force:

- What type of sales objectives are you setting for your product — sales units/dollars, market share, etc.? You may find it useful to use the A, B, C account type, single-factor model to set sales objectives.
- State the specific one-year objectives, broken down by control unit and calendarized.

	Control Unit A	Control Unit B	Control Unit C	Total
Quarter 1				
Quarter 2				
Quarter 3				
Quarter 4				
Total				

FIGURE 17B.1

SALES FORCE OBJECTIVES

C. DETERMINE AND ALLOCATE SALES FORCE SELLING EFFORT

In this exercise, you allocate selling effort to various customer groups and use your analysis to assess whether this effort level is appropriate for your product. In the first instance, you should use the A, B, C customer category, single-factor model (or the portfolio method if that seems more appropriate).

Use Figure 17C.1 to calculate amount of required selling time per year.

Customer Category, I	Sales Potential, II	Number of Customers, III	Selling Time Per Customer Annually, IV	Required Selling Time Annually, III × IV = V
A				
B				
C				
			Total	

FIGURE 17C.1

ESTIMATE OF REQUIRED SELLING TIME

Assess whether you are expending the appropriate level of selling effort. Calculate the required sales force size, using Figure 17C.2. Compare this figure with the actual sales force size. Explain the difference.

FIGURE 17C.2

CALCULATION OF
REQUIRED SALES
FORCE SIZE

Total required hours per year — Figure 17C.1	
Maximum selling time per salesperson (hours per year)	
Actual selling time per salesperson (hours per year)	
Number of salespeople required	
Actual number of salespeople	
Proposed firm/ business unit action	

Identify the time allocation for your sales force of the various activities you believe it should conduct — Figure 17C.3.

FIGURE 17C.3

IDENTIFY SALES FORCE
TIME ALLOCATION

Salesperson Activity	Time Allocation
Selling	
Traveling	
Administration	
Total	**100%**

D: SALES FORCE ORGANIZATION

In this section, you assess the organization of firm/business unit selling effort. Essentially, you should ask three questions.

- Should the selling effort be employee-based or outsourced?
- How should the selling effort be organized?
- Are there other approaches to addressing customers than an outside sales force model?

WHO DOES THE SELLING?
- For the product under consideration: Is your selling effort conducted by firm/business unit employees? Or is the selling effort outsourced to a third party?
- Are there any arguments in the context of your firm/business unit's situation that may lead you to consider a switch?

HOW IS THE SELLING EFFORT CURRENTLY ORGANIZED? Use Figure 17D.1. Note that in most cases, the firm/business unit will only be using one or two organizational forms.

Organizational Form	Current Organization	Proposed New Organization	Rational for Changing or Retaining
No geographic bounds			
Geographic			
Product			
Maintenance – new business			
Distribution channel			
Market segment			
Customer importance (strategy/key account)			
Other:			

FIGURE 17D.1

SALES FORCE ORGANIZATION

E. SALES FORCE PROCESSES

In this section you assess sales force processes and offer options for improvement.

Assess the following processes for directing and managing your firm/business unit's selling effort:
- Sales planning
- Pipeline analysis
- Sales forecasting
- Evaluation processes
- Reward systems

Use Figure 17E.1 to assess the current situation and to propose changes.

Sales Force Process	Current Assessment	Proposed Changes
Sales planning		
Pipeline analysis		
Sales forecasting		
Evaluation processes		
Reward systems		

FIGURE 17E.1

SALES FORCE PROCESSES

F. STAFFING THE SALES FORCE

Regardless of the other areas you examined in this chapter, if an employee-based outside sales effort is part of the implementation plan, you will need a well-trained, highly motivated sales force to be successful. To obtain such a sales force, you have to pay considerable attention to issues of recruiting, selecting, training, coaching, retaining, and replacing salespeople. You must be equally attentive to similar issues for sales managers.

Answer the following questions for salespeople — Figure 17F.1. Answer the same questions for sales managers — Figure 17F.2:
- How does your firm/business unit currently conduct this activity?
- How do you assess your firm/business unit's performance on this activity?
- What recommendations do you have for improving performance?

FIGURE 17F.1

STAFFING THE
SALES FORCE WITH
SALESPEOPLE

Activity	Current Method	Assessment	Recommendations
Recruiting			
Selecting			
Training			
Coaching			
Retaining			
Replacing			

FIGURE 17F.2

STAFFING THE
SALES FORCE WITH
SALES MANAGERS

Activity	Current Method	Assessment	Recommendations
Recruiting			
Selecting			
Training			
Coaching			
Retaining			
Replacing			

ANALYSIS CHECK

Make sure other decisions you made support, and are consistent with, sales force implementation:

- Is your sales force implementation supportive of the market strategy — Chapter 9?
- Is your sales force implementation supportive of the communications strategy — Chapter 15?
- Is your sales force implementation consistent with your mass and digital communications — Chapter 16?
- Is your sales force implementation consistent with other marketing implementation actions — Chapters 1, 13, 14, 15, 16, 18, 19, and 20?

Part C: Delivering Customer Value

CHAPTER 18: DISTRIBUTION DECISIONS

As noted in your textbook, well-developed distribution channels have greater longevity than other marketing mix elements. Nonetheless, the firm/business unit's distribution channel strategy must evolve, and may even have to change markedly. In this chapter, you examine the current distribution strategy for your product, analyze its strengths and deficiencies, and propose new distribution arrangements where desirable.

A. CURRENT DISTRIBUTION STRATEGY

- Use Figure 18A.1 to lay out current distribution arrangements for your target market segments. Use a boxes and arrows approach.

Target Segments	Target Segment:	Target Segment:	Target Segment:
Distribution system for reaching target segments			

FIGURE 18A.1

DIAGRAM CURRENT DISTRIBUTION SYSTEM

B. DISTRIBUTION CHANNEL FUNCTIONS

In this exercise, you focus on the various functions the distribution channel must conduct, and identify how well various distribution channel entities are performing.

DISTRIBUTION FUNCTIONS. Your distribution channel must fulfill a large number of functions. Select one of the market segments from Figure 18A.1 and identify which distribution channel entities conduct these functions. Use the material in your textbook to isolate the various functions of a distribution channel — Figure 18B.1. Repeat for other segments.

FIGURE 18B.1

DISTRIBUTION CHANNEL
FUNCTIONS AND
WHERE CONDUCTED

Segment: _____

Channel Entity	Functions Fulfilled	Channel Entity	Functions Fulfilled

DISTRIBUTION PERFORMANCE. In your distribution channel, there is probably a range of performance reflecting how well the various distribution channel entities fulfill these functions. Some of these functions will be performed well and others not so well. In Figure 18B.2, identify those functions that are performed well, those that need moderate improvement, and those that require major improvement.

FIGURE 18B.2

QUALITY OF CHANNEL
FUNCTION PERFORMANCE
AND IMPROVEMENT
OPTIONS

Segment: _____

Channel Functions Performed Well	Channel Functions Needing Moderate Improvement	Improvement Options	Channel Functions Needing Major Improvement	Improvement Options

Also, using Figure 18B.2, identify some ideas for improving performance on the functions you noted. When you develop these ideas, do not feel constrained by current distribution channel arrangements.

C. DISTRIBUTION CHANNEL DESIGN

Use results from the previous exercises to develop options and propose new distribution channel arrangements for your product:

- Develop several options for a new distribution channel design. Do not feel constrained by current distribution arrangements. Remember that evolving needs and wants of final customers should be primary in evaluating distribution arrangements, not current industry practice. Use Figure 18C.1 to sketch out your options.

Segment: _____

FIGURE 18C.1

OPTIONS FOR
NEW DISTRIBUTION
CHANNEL DESIGN

- Based on the options you developed in Figure 18C.1, lay out your proposed distribution channel design — Figure 18C.2. Note specifically where the various distribution functions will be conducted. In any new/modified design, there are going to be critical areas that managers must watch. If performance falls short in these areas, then performance in the entire system may be seriously affected.

Segment: _____

Proposed Design	Functions Fulfilled	Critical Issues to Watch

FIGURE 18C.2

PROPOSED DISTRIBUTION
CHANNEL DESIGN

ANALYSIS CHECK

Make sure prior analysis and other decisions support, and are consistent with, your distribution decisions:

- Are your distribution decisions consistent with insight you secured on customers — Chapter 4?
- Are your distribution decisions consistent with your market segmentation and targeting decisions — Chapter 8?
- Do your distribution decisions support the market strategy — Chapter 9?
- Are your distribution decisions consistent with other marketing implementation actions — Chapters 12, 13, 14, 15, 16, 19, and 20?

Part D: Getting Paid for Customer Value

CHAPTER 19: CRITICAL UNDERPINNINGS OF PRICING DECISIONS

In this chapter we focus on the underpinnings of pricing decisions. We begin by asking you to conduct a perceived-value analysis of your product compared with its competitors. We then suggest that you plot the positions of your product and your competitors on a price-value chart and relate the implications to your strategic objectives. Finally, consider what future pricing strategy and tactics might help you achieve the long-run objectives you established. (If delivery of economic value is critical to your value proposition, you should have completed the economic value analysis in Chapter 4, Section F. Use the results of that analysis to inform your pricing decisions.)

A. PERCEIVED-VALUE ANALYSIS

In Chapter 19 in your textbook, we developed a simple five-step model for conducting a perceived-value analysis. The example, shown in the chapter, analyzed three competitors producing easy chairs, assuming that the data was provided by experienced managers. Use the following instructions to complete Figure 19A.1 for your product. If you lack detailed knowledge of the product form/class, you may want to use inputs from managers or a sample of prospective customers. The steps are as follows:

1. Identify the benefits/values customers require, *excluding price.* You developed this list in Figure 8E.1 in Chapter 8. Enter in priority order in the left-hand column of Figure 19A.1. Remember that customers perceive value both in the product *and* in the supplier.

2. Assess the relative importance of each benefit/value to customers by assigning an importance weight such that the weights add up to 100.

3. Enter the names of your firm/business unit and major competitors from Section 5A — Chapter 5.

4. Taking the customer perspective, rate the perceived ability of the various competitive offers to deliver required benefits/values. For each competitive offer, rate its ability to deliver each benefit/value on a 1–10 scale: a score of "1" indicates the offer does not deliver the required benefit/value; a score of "10" indicates the offer delivers the benefit/value very well. Intermediate scores imply intermediate delivery levels.

5. For each competitor, multiply the importance weight for each benefit/value by that firm's rating.

6. For each competitor (including the firm/business unit), sum the products of the importance weights × ratings. The results depict the relative perceived value of the competing products in your category.

7. Write in the product prices for the firm/business unit and its competitors.

If you have any difficulty with this analysis, you may find it helpful to refer to the example in Chapter 19 of your textbook.

FIGURE 19A.1

PERCEIVED VALUE ANALYSIS

Required Benefits/ Values	Importance Weighting	Firm/Business Unit Price =		Competitor A Price =		Competitor B Price =		Competitor C Price =	
		Rate (1-10)	Total	Rate (1-10)	Total	Rate (1-10)	Total	Rate (1-10)	Total
	100	Grand Total		Grand Total		Grand Total		Grand Total	

B. MAPPING PRICE AND VALUE

Now you display the results of the perceived-value analysis and actual prices on a *customer value map*. By depicting relative value on the horizontal axis, and relative price on the vertical axis, we can graph value/price (V/P) positions for the various competitor suppliers. Use Figure 19B.1 for this purpose. Make your own decisions about scaling the axes.

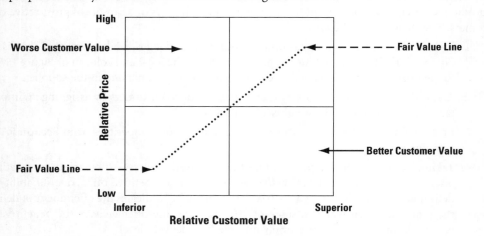

FIGURE 19B.1

CUSTOMER VALUE MAP

Ask yourself this question:

• Do the positions of the firm/business unit and competitors accurately reflect the market situation? Why? Or why not?

If your answer suggests you have an accurate depiction, ask the following questions:

- Is this the value/price position you wish your firm/business unit to occupy compared with competitors?
- How does this position fit with the strategic objectives you established for the product — Figure 9A.1 — Chapter 9?

CHAPTER 20: SETTING PRICES

Chapter 19 focused on the underpinnings of pricing decisions. Chapter 20 turns to the problem of actually setting prices.

A. THE PRICE-MAKING FRAMEWORK

An important element in price-setting is identifying the likely competitive response at different prices your firm/business unit is considering. In this exercise, you identify a variety of proposed prices and anticipate competitor responses. You then assess the likelihood that the firm/business unit will reach its objectives — Figure 20A.1.

FIGURE 20A.1

ANTICIPATING COMPETITIVE RESPONSE AND ACHIEVING FIRM/BUSINESS UNIT OBJECTIVES

Proposed Firm/ Business Unit Price	Anticipated Competitive Response	Likelihood of Reaching Firm/Business Unit Objective

B. MAKING PRICING DECISIONS

Finally, you should consider whether your product requires changes in pricing strategy or tactics. Use Figure 20B.1 to assist in these decisions.

FIGURE 20B.1

MAKING PRICING DECISIONS

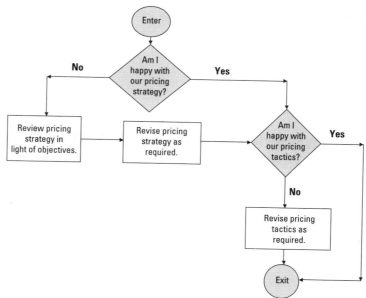

Remember, your strategic objectives should have a primary focus of growth/market share, profit, or cash flow. Does your pricing strategy align with your strategic objectives? If not, what modifications will you make? Once you are comfortable with your pricing strategy, consider whether you are making appropriate use of pricing tactics in the toolkit. We reproduce toolkit items from your textbook as Figure 20B.2 to prompt your thinking — Figure 20B.3.

Acceptable currency	Credit terms	Guarantees and warranties	Price stability
Allowances	Discounts	Inventory carrying costs	Slotting fees
Barter	Company shares	Leasing	Returns
Buy-backs	Freight	List price	Unbundling and bundling
Credit availability		Markdown money	

FIGURE: 20B.2

PRICING TOOLKIT

	Current	Proposed
Objectives		
Pricing Strategy		
Pricing Tactics		

FIGURE 20B.3

PRICING STRATEGY AND TACTICS

ANALYSIS CHECK

Make sure prior analysis and other decisions support, and are consistent with, your pricing recommendations:

- Are your pricing decisions reflective of your market insight — Chapter 3?
- Are your pricing decisions reflective of your customer insight — Chapter 4?
- Are your pricing decisions reflective of your competitor insight — Chapter 5?
- Is the pricing strategy supportive of the market strategy — Chapter 9?
- Do your pricing decisions capture the value you intend to deliver to customers — Chapter 9?

IMPERATIVE 5: *Secure Support from Other Functions*

CHAPTER 21: ENSURING THE FIRM IMPLEMENTS THE MARKET OFFER AS PLANNED

To ensure your strategies and implementation programs are executed as planned, you must align all functional areas in the firm/business unit so that employees embrace the notion that customers are central to firm/business unit success and act accordingly. In this chapter, we address the various elements you must consider in developing an external orientation.

A. INTER-FUNCTIONAL COORDINATION

A critical element to consider is the extent to which the marketing function interfaces with other functional areas in the firm/business unit. In this exercise, you identify the manner in which various functional areas interface with marketing, examine the quality of inter-functional interaction, and make recommendations for improvement — Figure 21A.1.

FIGURE 21A.1

INTER-FUNCTIONAL COORDINATION WITH MARKETING

Functional Area	Type of Interaction	Assessment of Coordination	Recommendations for Improvement
Customer service			
Finance			
Human resources			
Operations and the supply chain			
Research & development			
Sales			
Other			

B. FIRM/BUSINESS UNIT VALUES

Does your firm/business unit have a values statement that includes an expression of commitment to customers? Use Figure 21B.1 to answer the following questions:

- If your firm/business unit has a customer-focused values statement, report it here.
- Assess the positives and negatives of this statement.
- To what extent do you believe employees have internalized these values?
- How would you reframe the values statement?
- What actions would you take to gain greater commitment to your reframed values statement?

FIGURE 21B.1

VALUES STATEMENT

Values Statement	Positives	Negatives	Reframed Values Statement	Suggested Actions to Gain Commitment

C. MARKETING ORGANIZATION

In this exercise, you examine the line organization for marketing.

- Sketch out the line organization for marketing in your firm/business unit — Figure 21C.1.

Examining your firm/business unit's marketing organization:

- What are the positive features of this organization?
- What are the negative features of this organization?
- What actions do you recommend to improve the line organization for marketing?
- Why do you think your recommendations will improve the situation?

Report your answers to these questions in Figure 21C.2

Positive Features	Negative Features
Recommendations	**Why the Recommendations Will Work**

D. SYSTEMS AND PROCESSES

Systems and processes are important in ensuring the firm/business unit conducts its marketing appropriately. Chapter 21 in your textbook distinguishes between *hard* systems and *soft* systems.

In this exercise you should identify *hard* systems and *soft* systems that support making the firm/business unit more externally oriented. Identify these systems and discuss their pros and cons. What other systems and processes do you think your firm/business unit should introduce to become more externally focused? — Figure 21D.1.

FIGURE 21D.1

SYSTEMS AND PROCESSES

Type of System	Description	Pros and Cons	Proposed Changes
Hard system: Current			
Hard system: New			
Soft system: Current			
Soft system: New			

E. HUMAN RESOURCE MANAGEMENT

Work in organizations is done by people. To build an externally oriented, market-responsive organization, requires the right sort of people. In this exercise, you assess the quality of the firm/business unit's workforce management systems for ensuring you have the *right* people in the *right* positions — Figure 21E.1.

- How do you assess your firm/business unit's workforce management practices as regards marketing? What are the positive features? What are the negative features?
- What suggestions do you have for improvements?

FIGURE 21E.1

ASSESSING WORKFORCE MANAGEMENT SYSTEMS

Workforce Management Practices	Positives	Negatives	Suggestions for Improvement

F. SUSTAINING AN EXTERNAL ORIENTATION

Chapter 21 in your textbook discusses several potential impediments to sustaining an external orientation. We identified these impediments as:

- Accounting systems
- Bureaucracy
- Centralization versus decentralization
- Excessive focus on organizational efficiency
- Functional divisions
- Functional view of marketing
- Internal politics
- Inward-oriented marketing departments
- Misaligned incentives
- Social fabric of institutions

Assess your firm/business unit's situation on these various dimensions — Figure 21F.1. What suggestions do you have for improving organizational effectiveness?

Dimension of Impediment	Current Situation	Suggestions for Improvement
Accounting systems		
Bureaucracy		
Centralization versus decentralization		
Excessive focus on organizational efficiency		
Functional divisions		
Functional view of marketing		
Internal politics		
Inward-oriented marketing department		
Misaligned incentives		
Social fabric of the institution		

FIGURE 21F.1

EXAMINING THE
MARKETING
ORGANIZATION

ANALYSIS CHECK

Make sure your recommendations for implementing the marketing offer are likely to be successful:

- Are your recommendations consistent with the market strategy — Chapter 9?
- Are your recommendations consistent with your decisions to implement the market strategy — Chapters 12, 13, 14, 15, 16, 17, 18, 19, and 20?

IMPERATIVE 6: *Monitor and Control*

CHAPTER 22: MONITORING AND CONTROLLING FIRM FUNCTIONING AND PERFORMANCE

In this chapter we focus on monitoring and controlling performance. We begin by asking you to review the system your firm/business unit currently uses to monitor and control performance. We then ask you to briefly address firm/business unit functioning as a whole.

A. PERFORMANCE CONTROL

The first task is specifically focused on your product. Remember that performance control asks: Given the action(s) taken by the firm/business unit, were the planned results achieved? Chapter 22 of your textbook raises several important issues regarding the metrics used by many firms. We suggest that the metrics are sometimes deficient because they neglect the principles of steering control: hence, leading indicators are not used. Similarly, some firms fail to apply the accountability principle, so that some employees are inappropriately evaluated on measures over which they have little or no control. We assume you are looking at the appropriate organizational level within your firm/business unit and will use the input-intermediate-output approach to analyze the performance-control system.

Input measures focus on actions taken by the firm/business unit. Most intermediate measures focus on actions customers take that should lead to firm/business unit outputs, but are not themselves outputs. Output measures are the most conventional performance-control measures and include variables like sales revenues and profits. In a cause-and-effect relationship, inputs lead to intermediates; in turn, intermediates lead to outputs — Figure 22A.1. You must link firm/business unit actions — inputs — with output performance. Intermediate variables are often the key element in establishing such linkages. Implementing a steering-control philosophy, both input and intermediate measures should provide leading indicators of output changes.

FIGURE 22A.1

RELATIONSHIPS AMONG CONTROL MEASURES

This exercise asks you to identify what input, intermediate, and output measures your firm/business unit uses for performance control of your product. You may find there are deficiencies. Deficiencies typically occur in the absence or under-representation of input and intermediate measures; hence, the firm/business unit cannot adequately practice steering control because it lacks leading indicators. Also, firms sometimes do not reflect their strategic objectives in the choice of output measures; make sure there is a correspondence for your product.

Chapter 22 in your textbook contains numerous examples of input, intermediate, and output measures, comprising both *hard* and *soft* metrics. We ask you to recommend measures to correct any deficiencies you observe — Figure 22A.2.

FIGURE 22A.2

ASSESSING PERFORMANCE CONTROL MEASURES

Type of Measures	Input Measures	Intermediate Measures	Output Measures
Measures now used			
Suggested changes/ additions			

In designing a monitor-and-control process, you should pursue several steps:

1. **Identify the process to control.** Managers clarify the focus of the control system.

2. **Decide and define measures.** The firm/business unit decides what to measure — input, intermediate, output variables. The firm/business unit also decides when to measure and devises a process for developing standards.

3. **Develop a measurement system.** Managers figure out the appropriate systems to collect, integrate, and analyze relevant data, and how to distribute results to managers who need them.

4. **Set standards.** The firm/business unit decides what standards to apply for each measure. In general, standards should flow from action programs developed as part of the market strategy — Chapter 9.

5. **Measure results.** Using the measurement system developed in step 3, the firm/business unit collects, integrates, analyzes, and distributes results.

6. **Compare results against standards; identify gaps and variances.** Managers compare results (step 5) against standards (step 4) to identify performance gaps.

7. **Understand and communicate performance gaps.** Performance gap information, and its interpretation, is communicated to those responsible for taking action. Some gaps may be positive — firm/business unit performance exceeds standards; other gaps may be negative — firm performance is inferior to standards.

8. **Generate and evaluate alternatives.** Managers identify alternative actions to close negative gaps. If the standards were well set, negative gaps most likely require corrective action. Positive gaps may indicate performance standards should be set higher. Managers should always question if the original standards were appropriate.

9. **Select alternative and take action.** Managers select an alternative, then develop and implement an action plan.

You should be clear that you are focusing on your product, but these steps highlight the fact that monitor and control is an ongoing process, not a one-time event. You should be aware that, as with other aspects of your strategy and tactics, you may face significant implementation problems when attempting to act upon your recommendations.

FINANCIAL PERFORMANCE One output you will want to measure is financial performance. We prefer a contribution-oriented approach. Figure 22A.3 provides a template for financial performance projections based on a contribution-oriented system. (If contribution margin data are not available, develop income statements using the template in Figure PA.1 in the Preamble.)

	Year 0	Year 1	Year 2	Year 3	Year 4	Year 5
Sales Revenues						
Variable Costs						
Contribution Margin						
Direct Fixed Costs						
Indirect Fixed Costs						
Total Fixed Costs						
Net Profit						

FIGURE 22A.3

PROJECTED FINANCIAL RESULTS

B. FIRM FUNCTIONING CONTROL

Firm functioning control comprises three aspects:

- **Implementation control.** Did the firm/business unit implement planned actions?
- **Strategy control.** Is the firm/business unit's market strategy well conceived and on target?
- **Managerial process control.** Are the firm/business unit's processes the best they can be?

In this exercise we ask you to briefly review each aspect.

IMPLEMENTATION CONTROL Implementation control concerns whether or not the firm/business unit implemented its planned actions. Identify the previous period's market strategy and plan and determine whether or not planned actions were implemented. If there were difficulties:

- Were the difficulties external? External difficulties suggest a failure to predict market conditions sufficiently accurately (a planning and forecasting problem).
- Were the difficulties internal? Internal problems suggest problems of implementation control.

In either case, what are your suggestions to remedy the situation? — Figure 22B.1.

FIGURE 22B.1

ASSESSING IMPLEMENTATION CONTROL

	Difficulties	Suggestions
External		
Internal		

STRATEGY CONTROL. Strategy control concerns whether or not the firm/business unit's market strategy is well conceived and on target. One way to assess strategy quality is to examine the significance of changes you recommend.

- Are the changes you recommended a consequence of changed market conditions?
- Are the changes you recommended based on your diagnosis of problems with strategy control?
- If the problems are in strategy control, how could you avoid them in the future? — Figure 22B.2.

FIGURE 22B.2

ASSESSING STRATEGY CONTROL

	Market Strategy Changes Based on:	Potential Actions to Avoid Future Problems with Strategy Control
Changed Market Conditions		
Problems with Strategy Control		

MANAGERIAL PROCESS CONTROL By now, you should have a pretty good idea of whether or not your firm/business unit is world-class in managerial processes. Where you find deficiencies, you should suggest remedial steps — Figure 22B.3.

Problem Observed	Re-engineering Approach?	Best Practice Approach?	Benchmarking Approach?	Other: Please Indicate

FIGURE 22B.3

ASSESSING MANAGERIAL PROCESS CONTROL

ANALYSIS CHECK

Make certain your monitor and control system will be effective for both performance and firm/business unit functioning.

Managing Marketing in the 21ˢᵗ Century

SECTION I: MARKETING AND THE FIRM

CHAPTER 1
Introduction to Managing Marketing

CHAPTER 2
The Value of Customers

SECTION II: FUNDAMENTAL INSIGHTS FOR STRATEGIC MARKETING

CHAPTER 3
Market Insight

CHAPTER 4
Customer Insight

CHAPTER 6
Marketing Research

CHAPTER 5
Insight about Competitors, Company, and Complementers

SECTION III: STRATEGIC MARKETING

IMPERATIVE 1
Determine and Recommend Which Markets to Address

CHAPTER 7
Identifying and Choosing Opportunities

IMPERATIVE 2
Identify and Target Market Segments

CHAPTER 8
Market Segmentation and Targeting

IMPERATIVE 3
Set Strategic Direction and Positioning

CHAPTER 9
Market Strategy: Integrating Firm Efforts for Marketing Success

CHAPTER 10
Managing through the Life Cycle

CHAPTER 11
Managing Brands

SECTION IV: IMPLEMENTING THE MARKET STRATEGY

IMPERATIVE 4
Design the Market Offer

PART A: PROVIDING CUSTOMER VALUE

PART B: COMMUNICATING CUSTOMER VALUE

PART C: DELIVERING CUSTOMER VALUE

PART D: GETTING PAID FOR CUSTOMER VALUE

CHAPTER 12
Managing the Product Line

CHAPTER 15
Integrated Marketing Communications

CHAPTER 18
Distribution Decisions

CHAPTER 19
Critical Underpinnings of Pricing Decisions

CHAPTER 13
Managing Services and Customer Service

CHAPTER 16
Mass and Digital Communication

CHAPTER 20
Setting Prices

CHAPTER 14
Developing New Products

CHAPTER 17
Directing and Managing the Field Sales Effort

IMPERATIVE 5
Secure Support from Other Functions

CHAPTER 21
Ensuring the Firm Implements the Market Offer as Planned

IMPERATIVE 6
Monitor and Control

CHAPTER 22
Monitoring and Controlling Firm Functioning and Performance

SECTION V: SPECIAL MARKETING TOPICS

CHAPTER 23
International, Regional, and Global Marketing

Section V: Special Marketing Topics

CHAPTER 23: INTERNATIONAL, REGIONAL, AND GLOBAL MARKETING

In this chapter, we focus on the firm/business unit's decision to enter a foreign market(s).

A. COUNTRY ATTRACTIVENESS ANALYSIS

The approach for determining the attractiveness of various countries to enter is virtually identical to the method presented in Chapter 8 for assessing the attractiveness of various market segments. The only difference is that in this case, the segments are individual countries. You develop a chart similar to Figure 23A.1. The five steps for assessing country attractiveness are:

1. **Factor identification.** Identify general factors of country attractiveness for your firm/business unit. Examples are — large population, currency stability, low levels of government regulation, and degree of corruption. Complete the following statement: "Given our history, objectives, culture, management style, successes, and failures, we like to operate in countries that offer … ." Brainstorm these factors — Figure 23A.2. When you have completed brainstorming, combine or eliminate factors until you have from five to eight factors. Enter these factors in Figure 23A.2. Describe why you included each factor. Also enter these factors in the far left column of Figure 23A.3.

Attractiveness Factors	Importance Weight (I)	Great Britain Rating (RA) (1 to 10 scale)	Australia Rating (RB) (1 to 10 scale)	Mexico Rating (RC) (1 to 10 scale)	Great Britain I × RA	Australia I × RB	Mexico I × RC
1 Market size	30	8	3	5	240	90	150
2 Growth potential	20	5	7	8	100	140	160
3 Communications ease	10	10	10	3	100	100	30
4 Travel ease	10	5	2	9	50	20	90
5 Currency stability	10	7	7	4	70	70	40
6 Firm learning	10	3	3	8	30	30	80
7 Degree of corruption	10	8	8	5	80	80	50
	100				**Σ670**	**Σ530**	**Σ600**

FIGURE 23A.1

COMPLETED COUNTRY ATTRACTIVENESS ANALYSIS

2. **Factor weighting.** Weight each factor in Figure 23A.3 by allocating 100 points based on its importance to the firm/business unit. Factor weights should add up to 100. Note that these two steps do not involve any analysis of countries. The responses are specific to your firm/business unit for analysis of many country opportunities.

Now, along the top of Figure 23A.3, write in the various countries you are considering entering. Select the first country for analysis. You repeat the analysis for additional countries.

FIGURE 23A.2

SELECTED COUNTRY ATTRACTIVENESS FACTORS AND REASONS TO INCLUDE

Attractiveness Factors	Reasons to Include

FIGURE 23A.3

COUNTRY ATTRACTIVENESS ANALYSIS

Attractiveness Factors	Importance Weight (I)	Country 1 Rating (RA) (1 to 10 scale)	Country 2 Rating (RB) (1 to 10 scale)	Country 3 Rating (RC) (1 to 10 scale)	Country 1 I × RA	Country 2 I × RB	Country 3 I × RC
1							
2							
3							
4							
5							
6							
7							
	100				___	___	___

3. **Country opportunity rating.** In Figure 23A.3, select one country. For each *factor*, provide a **rating** score, on a 1 to 10 scale, based on the extent to which the country conforms to that factor. A score of "1" implies the country does not conform to the factor; a score of "10" implies high conformance. For example if the criterion is high population, a score of "1" implies the country population is small; a score of "10" implies the country has a large population. Scores from 2 to 9 imply intermediate population sizes.

4. **Develop factor scores.** In Figure 23A.3, for each factor, multiply the *factor weighting* by the *country-specific rating*.

5. **Country attractiveness score.** In Figure 23A.3, sum the *factor scores* from step 4. This **total** number is the *country attractiveness* score; the range is 100 to 1,000.

6. Repeat steps 3 through 5 for the other countries.

Note: In step 3, we suggest you perform the ratings one country at a time, across factors. You may find it easier to complete the rating task one factor at a time, across countries.

B. BUSINESS STRENGTHS ANALYSIS

To complete the analysis for deciding whether or not to enter a country, the firm/business unit should assess its chances of success. The process for completing this analysis is identical to the analysis in Chapter 8, Section G — Business Strengths Analysis, comprising Figures 8G.1, 8G.2, and 8G.3. We reproduce these figures (slightly modified) — Figures 23B.1, 23B.2, 23B.3.

Country:

1. _____
2. _____
3. _____
4. _____
5. _____
6. _____
7. _____
8. _____
9. _____
10. _____

Country:

1. _____
2. _____
3. _____
4. _____
5. _____
6. _____
7. _____
8. _____
9. _____
10. _____

FIGURE 23B.1

**BRAINSTORM
BUSINESS
STRENGTHS
FACTORS**

Country:

Business Strengths Factor	Reason to Include
1.	
2.	
3.	
4.	
5.	
6.	
7.	
8.	

Country:

Business Strengths Factor	Reason to Include
1.	
2.	
3.	
4.	
5.	
6.	
7.	
8.	

FIGURE 23B.2

**SELECTED BUSINESS
STRENGTHS FACTORS
AND REASONS
TO INCLUDE**

FIGURE 23B.3

BUSINESS STRENGTHS ANALYSIS

Country:

Factor	Weight	Rate	Total
	100	Total	

Country:

Factor	Weight	Rate	Total
	100	Total	

C. MATRIX REPRESENTATION

You should combine the results from the Country Attractiveness Analysis (A) and Business Strengths Analysis (B) to form the Matrix Representation, similar to Figure 8H.1 — Figure 23C.1.

FIGURE 23C.1

COUNTRY ATTRACTIVENESS/ BUSINESS STRENGTHS MATRIX

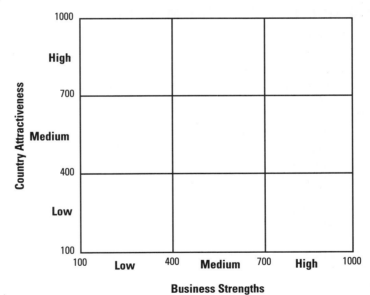

D. OPTIONS FOR ENTERING FOREIGN MARKETS

Your textbook identified several methods for entering foreign markets. From the matrix representation of countries in Section C, you should identify those countries you will consider entering. Using Figure 23D.1, identify the pros and cons of the various options for entering the first country. Repeat for additional countries.

Country: _____

Entry Method	Pros	Cons
Passive Entry		
Exporting		
Licensing		
Active Entry		
Importing		
Local production		
Acquisition		
Greenfield		
Joint venture		
Franchising		

Decision: _____

FIGURE 23D.1

ANALYSIS OF FOREIGN MARKET ENTRY OPTIONS

E. SEGMENTING MULTIPLE COUNTRY MARKETS

Your textbook identifies two broad approaches for segmenting country markets — grouping similar countries — Figure 23E.1 — and across-country segmentation like the Roper Starch Worldwide system — Strivers, Devouts, Altruists, Intimates, Fun seekers, and Creatives. Use Figure 23E.2 to identify the segmentation approach you intend to use, and identify specific segments.

Anglo	Arab	Far Eastern	Germanic	Latin American	Latin European	Near Eastern	Nordic	Independents
Australia	Bahrain	Indonesia	Austria	Argentina	Belgium	Greece	Denmark	Brazil
Canada	Kuwait	Hong Kong	Germany	Chile	France	Iran	Finland	India
Great Britain	Oman	Malaysia	Switzerland	Colombia	Italy	Turkey	Norway	Israel
Ireland	United Arab Emirates	Philippines		Mexico	Portugal		Sweden	Japan
New Zealand	Saudi Arabia	Singapore		Peru	Spain			
South Africa		Taiwan		Venezuela				
United States								

FIGURE 23E.1

COUNTRIES GROUPED BY ATTITUDINAL SIMILARITY

	Grouping Countries	Across-Country Segmentation
Segmentation Approach	Yes / No	Yes / No
Segments		

FIGURE 23E.2

SEGMENTING MULTI-COUNTRY MARKETS

EXECUTIVE SUMMARY

In your finished document, the executive summary comes first, but is the final item you write, after you complete work on all the chapters. The executive summary should provide a brief, concise, yet complete view of the results of your analysis. The executive summary should be action-oriented in terms of what you believe the organization should do as the result of your efforts.

Give serious thought as to how you will present your work to busy senior executives who may read only the executive summary. They may never delve deeply into the project, or may concentrate only on a particular item that interests them. What follows is one way of organizing a series of paragraphs in the executive summary and the source of material that may work for you. At the very least, this framework provides you with a jumping-off point to develop your own presentation structure.

1. **Opening Paragraph** — What this project is all about – Preamble and Chapter 1
2. **Market, Customer, and Competitor Insight** — Chapters 2, 3, 4, 5, and 6
3. **Key Assumptions** — Transition to Strategic Marketing
4. **Imperative 1: Determine and Recommend Which Markets to Address** — Chapter 7
5. **Imperative 2: Identify and Target Market Segments** — Chapter 8
6. **Imperative 3: Set Strategic Direction and Positioning** — Chapters 9, 10, and 11
7. **Imperative 4: Design the Market Offer** — Chapters 12, 13, 14, 15, 16, 17, 18, 19, and 20
8. **Imperative 5: Secure Support from Other Functions** — Chapter 21
9. **Imperative 6: Monitor and Control** — Chapter 22
10. **International, Regional, and Global Marketing** — Chapter 23

APPENDIX 1: MARKET PLANS DEVELOPED USING *THE VIRGIN MARKETER*

COMPANY	COMPETITIVE ARENA	COMPANY	COMPETITIVE ARENA
Abbott Vascular	Coronary treatments	Joie de Vivre	Urban resort
Akimbo Systems	Video on demand	Kent Imaging Systems	Medical imaging
Animal and Bird Medical Center of Temple (Texas)	Animal care	La Jolla Digital	Software
Bone Cancer Research Foundation	Not-for-profit foundation	Leapfrog	Toys
Case Central	Litigation support	LexisNexis	Online information
Climate Trust	Carbon emission offsets	Moet & Chandon	Sparkling wines
Columbia-Berkeley Executive MBA Program	Education	AskJeeves	Internet site
Digital Technology International	Printed publication services	MOVA	Movie animation
eBay	Online marketplace	Oakland Animal Shelter	Animal care
Genesis Microchip	Display image processors	Office Depot	Office supplies
Generics Yes!	Pharmaceuticals	PepsiCo	Water
Hall Wines	Vineyards	Risk Management Solutions	Software
Hambrecht and Co	IPOs	Ristarose	Wedding gowns
Hammerhead Systems	Telecommunications	TurboTools	Productivity software
Hewlett-Packard	Digital photography	Turn	Online advertising
Industrial Light & Magic	Movie visual effects	Vine Connections	Wine importer
Intel	Microprocessors	World Wrapps	Franchised restaurants

APPENDIX 2: ENHANCING YOUR OWN HUMAN CAPITAL

To complete *The Virgin Marketer* project will take several weeks of dedication by you and your group members. Your personal experience during this effort can form the basis for improving your own effectiveness and that of your colleagues. In the following pages, we provide some simple templates to help you achieve these goals. We hope you decide to use them.

APPLICATION IDEAS. As you work through *The Virgin Marketer* project, you will have ideas that you may apply in your job or in your other courses. Don't lose these ideas; write them down as they occur to you. Recall that two-time Nobel laureate Linus Pauling said that the best way to get a good idea was to have a lot of ideas. Figure A2.1 gives you space to write down each idea. You can also assess whether it would be easy or hard to apply and whether the payoff for implementation would be high or low.

LEARNING AND PERSONAL DEVELOPMENT. While you are working on *The Virgin Marketer* project, you will realize there are things you don't know that you would like to know. The pressures of class and work may make it difficult to secure these right away. Figure A2.2 gives you space to identify topics, specify the resources that each item may require, and identify the potential payoff both to you personally and to your current or future employer. Write them down as they occur to you.

PERSONAL INSIGHTS ABOUT YOU AND YOUR GROUP MEMBERS. During *The Virgin Marketer* project, you will be working extensively with colleagues. Figure A2.3 asks questions about personal style, learning, working with others, and leading and managing. When the project is complete, we suggest that each group member fill out a template for every other group member, including himself/herself. These data provide useful 360-degree feedback. Figure A2.4 provides an example. (If you are concerned about confidentiality, you could give the templates to a third party to make summaries for each of you.)

PERSONAL ACTION PLAN AGENDA. The application ideas, learning and personal development, and personal insights form the raw material from which to develop a personal action planning agenda. You will discard some items, combine two or more items to make a new item, and elaborate others. Figure A2.5 provides space for you to articulate your specific personal agenda for the next 12 months and to identify individual action items. You should note the level of importance of each item and the degree of urgency.

FIGURE A2.1

APPLICATION IDEAS

List specific ideas for applying what you learned in your work situation.

FIGURE A2.2

LEARNING AND PERSONAL DEVELOPMENT

List topics/areas for your individual development.

Topic/Area	Potential Resources	Payoff
		Low High Easy Hard
		Low High Easy Hard
		Low High Easy Hard
		Low High Easy Hard
		Low High Easy Hard
		Low High Easy Hard
		Low High Easy Hard
		Low High Easy Hard
		Low High Easy Hard
		Low High Easy Hard
		Low High Easy Hard
		Low High Easy Hard
		Low High Easy Hard
		Low High Easy Hard
		Low High Easy Hard
		Low High Easy Hard
		Low High Easy Hard
		Low High Easy Hard

FIGURE A2.3

PERSONAL INSIGHTS ABOUT YOU AND YOUR GROUP MEMBERS

Group Member:

Personal Style/Approach

Learning Approach

Working with Others

Leading and Managing

Group Member:

Personal Style/Approach

Learning Approach

Working with Others

Leading and Managing

Group Member:

FIGURE A2.3

(CONTINUED)

Personal Style/Approach

Learning Approach

Working with Others

Leading and Managing

Group Member:

Personal Style/Approach

Learning Approach

Working with Others

Leading and Managing

FIGURE A2.3

(CONTINUED)

FIGURE A2.4

EXAMPLE OF PERSONAL INSIGHTS ABOUT YOU AND YOUR GROUP MEMBERS

Group Member:

Personal Style/Approach

She seems to be a right-brain thinker, analytical and linear, working from the big picture to the details. She misses opportunities to be more creative or nontraditional in her approach and in her thinking.

Learning Approach

He seems to learn best when he has a model or framework on which to hang the details. He seems to find it difficult to concentrate on discussions or issues when he doesn't understand the concepts behind them.

Working with Others

When she's in a group, she tends to lie back and wait for someone else to take the lead. She waits until the group is well into the discussion and others have taken a stand before she makes her own points.

Leading and Managing

I take too long when working with the group to tell them my ideas. When I am chair, the meetings are too long and unfocused. I don't think that group members understand my decision-making process.

My specific personal goals for the next 12 months are:

Given these personal goals, my action planning agenda is:

Action Item

Urgent / Yes / No — Important / No Yes (repeated for each action item row)

ENDNOTES

1. A.K. Kohli, B.J. Jaworski, and A. Kumar, "MARKOR: A Measure of Market Orientation," *Journal of Marketing Research*, 30 (November 1993), pp. 467–477.

2. The MARKOR scale has been tested for reliability and validity. We make no claims for scaling properties of the scales we use here. However, we do believe that the instrument has superior diagnostic power.

3. You may complete this analysis against the competitive set as a whole, or against individual competitors.